699

MW01264658

Forget-Me-Not Lane

Miriam's Journal
A Fruitful Vine
A Winding Path
A Joyous Heart
A Treasured Friendship
A Golden Sunbeam

Joy's Journal
Tall Cedars Homestead
Beechwood Acres
Majestic Oak Memoirs
Forget-Me-Not Lane

Miriam Joy, who now goes by the name Joy, was just a little girl in the "Miriam's Journal series." In Joy's Journal, she marries Kermit, moves first to Tall Cedars Homestead, then to Beechwood Acres, reminisces in Majestic Oak Memoirs, and now takes us up Forget-Me-Not Lane.

Joy's Journal #4

Forget-Me-Not Lane

Carrie Bender

Masthof Press
219 Mill Road
Morgantown, PA 19543-9516

FORGET-ME-NOT LANE

Copyright © 2004

Cover artwork
by Julie Stauffer Martin, Ephrata, Pa.

✦ ✦ ✦ ✦ ✦

Sketches in text
by Julie Stauffer Martin

Golden Gems are taken from
Day By Day With Andrew Murray
compiled by M.J. Shepperson in 1961 and reprinted with
permission of Bethany House Publishers.
All rights reserved.

Library of Congress Control Number: 2003116859
International Standard Book Number: 1-930353-59-6

Published 2004
Masthof Press
219 Mill Road
Morgantown, PA 19543-9516

This story is fiction.
Parts are based on actual happenings,
but not always in the correct time
they occurred.

Contents

———————————

The Forget-Me-Not plant contains
clusters of small blue, white, or pink flowers—
an emblem of faithfulness and friendship.

———————————

Part One

Motherhood Blessings

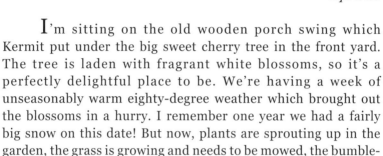

I'm sitting on the old wooden porch swing which Kermit put under the big sweet cherry tree in the front yard. The tree is laden with fragrant white blossoms, so it's a perfectly delightful place to be. We're having a week of unseasonably warm eighty-degree weather which brought out the blossoms in a hurry. I remember one year we had a fairly big snow on this date! But now, plants are sprouting up in the garden, the grass is growing and needs to be mowed, the bumblebees are buzzing, and the birds are singing joyously.

I haven't gotten around to starting my new journal until today because we were so busy getting settled after we moved here in March. We live just across the creek from Aunt Miriam and Uncle Nate. It's not more than one-third of a mile if we go through Forget-Me-Not Lane, as my friend Sadie so aptly named it. The lane goes through their orchard, winds down to the creek where we have to cross on a series of stepping stones, then continues through the meadow and through our pine grove. Their place is really close, but we can't see each other because of the pines and other trees.

When Aunt Miriam comes over, she goes the long way around, over the *Ketta Shtake* (swinging bridge) rather than over the stones in the creek, but Sadie and I go back and forth the nearest way.

Even before we moved here, Sadie had named the path Forget-Me-Not Lane because of the blooming forget-me-nots by the wayside. Since we've come, Sadie says the name is more fitting than ever because the forget-me-not is an emblem of faithfulness and friendship. To my way of thinking, Sadie herself is an emblem of faithfulness and friendship. She has proved to be a real friend.

We haven't thought of a name for our place yet. Kermit jokingly suggested Forget-Me-Not Farmette, but that sounds too silly. Perhaps we'll just call it Kermit's Woodworking Shop, because that has been his livelihood the few weeks we've been here. There are only five acres to this place and we plan to sell some produce this summer. I'll describe our house next time because it's time to get supper on the table. I rest whenever I feel like it these days, because that's what the midwife told me to do. I'm counting the weeks until June!

I think I'll take the time to quickly copy a Golden Gem for Today.

> **Golden Gem for today:** *Abiding in God's love cleanses the heart from selfishness, purifies the heart's motives, and strengthens the heart's character.*

April 21

I spent the forenoon in the woodworking shop, helping Kermit with the sanding. He's making beautiful oak kitchen cabinets which were ordered for somebody's dream kitchen. Maybe someday when we have a house of our own, he will make some like that for me.

Buying all the woodworking equipment and lumber was a big investment, so we'll have to live frugally for awhile. Business is picking up, though, for while I was in the shop, a young bride-to-be came in to order a new bedroom suite, a twenty-foot kitchen table, and a dozen chairs! Kermit was so pleased.

Now I'll describe our farmette. Our house is a rambling old, gray-shingled farmhouse with a wide front porch—nearly as big as our L-shaped porch at Beechwood Acres. The kitchen is comfortable and roomy, with white kitchen cabinets, blue-checkered linoleum, and trailing green ivy stenciling. The living room has a broad window seat under a big bay window. I plan to make a nice cushion for it as soon as I get around to it. The walls are paneled half-way up with cedar paneling, and the upper half is lavender-flowered vinyl wall covering. The *Commar* (downstairs bedroom) has blue-flowered wallpaper with a border of delphiniums along the top. The rooms upstairs aren't very nice at all— the wallpaper needs to be replaced and the paint is chipping off. But for now we'll leave it as it is, because I don't feel like tackling any major decorating jobs.

Outbuildings include a small horse barn and carriage shed and the big shop where Kermit does his woodworking. Besides the big sweet cherry tree in the front yard and the pine grove, there are two big birch trees, an old pear tree, and several apple trees. Along the stony, winding lane leading out to the road, there are various kinds of trees in all sizes and shapes—wild junipers, willows, poplars, and scraggly-looking Siberian elms blocking our view of the road. It's not a showplace, but so far we like it here. We're close to nature and away from the noise of traffic. Be it ever so humble, it's Home Sweet Home.

Ya well, I must go whip up an angel food cake with the egg whites left over from noodle-making. I'll take the time, though, to copy an inspirational verse:

> *We are thirsty, Lord, and we long for the refresh-*
> *ment only You can give. May we not settle for the tem-*
> *porary satisfaction the world offers, but reach for the*
> *living water only You can give.*
> *"Whosoever drinketh of the water that I shall give*
> *him shall never thirst; but the water that I shall give*
> *him shall be in him a well of water springing up into*
> *everlasting life." (John 4:14)*

April 22

There's a cardinal whistling, "Good cheer, good cheer, good cheer" from the pine grove, and a pair of robins are starting to build a nest in the apple tree by the carriage shed, singing joyously and wholeheartedly, morning, noon, and night! The cherry tree is still a breathtakingly splendid maze of glorious white blossoms, and sitting on the creaking old porch swing is an exquisite experience. It's too bad the blossoms last only a few days.

This morning, Sadie came traipsing down Forget-Me-Not Lane as blithely as a schoolgirl, bringing a bag of freshly-baked molasses cookies and staying to chat awhile. When she saw that I was ready to plant my sweet corn, Sadie rolled up her sleeves and got right to work making the rows. She's the kind of person who spreads joy: her coming is like a cheerful warmth; she passes by and we are content; she stays awhile and we are happy; her presence lights up our day. I'm so glad we live close to each other.

Kermit needs a helper in the woodworking shop, so we have written to the Millers in Montana, asking if Jared can come. We knew we would have been able to get someone nearby to be our *Gnecht* (hired boy) this summer, but we've grown quite attached to Jared. The Millers were originally from Pennsylvania, and since Jared made the remark that he wanted to come back to do his *rumshpringing* someday, we were bold enough to ask.

We received a letter from the Millers today saying that there is a van load of people coming this way in May, and Jared will be coming along! While reading the letter, I got another bright idea. Why not ask his cousin, Treva Mullet, to come along and be my "mother's helper" when the baby arrives? I have a letter to them all ready to mail tomorrow, and I can hardly wait to hear from them. I know Mom would send Sis over to help, but they're so busy with the babies they are caring for (babies whose mothers are in prison) that I don't like to ask.

Time to go wash the carriage, for we want to hitch up and go see my family tonight.

> ***Golden Gem for today:*** *A wife is to reverence her husband. That means submit to him, notice him, prefer him, esteem him, regard him and what he says, venerate him, or make much of his worth, admire him exceedingly—all these things are wrapped up in the word "reverence."*

While writing that, I thought of what friend Jill of our Tall Cedars Homestead days said: She would never promise to obey her husband, Wynn. But according to the Bible, wives are to submit to their husbands "as unto the Lord," or as though the Lord stood in the husband's place. That is a thought-provoking statement.

Prayer For A Bride

By her beautiful character, her consistent Christian example, and her earnest application of the homemaking arts, may her home be a haven of peace and contentment, dear Lord. Amen.

Aunt Miriam walked over last night (by way of the swinging bridge), bringing a bunch of watercress she found in the spring water. Yum—watercress sandwiches!

She cheered up my evening, for I was feeling so remorseful about something I did. I didn't tell her about it because I am sure she wouldn't have done what I did.

Let me explain. Our financial situation is in such dire straits just now because our investments haven't brought in any returns yet. I keep track of every penny I spend and have to scrimp and save and do without, and I buy only the barest necessities. Sometimes I feel so rebellious about it that I splurge anyway, against my better judgement and much to my regret later on.

It is to my shame that I write about what I did yesterday—how I wish I could undo it, but it is too late now. I was sitting on the porch with my feet elevated (midwife's orders) when a shiny, new-looking car drove in the lane.

A man got out, walked toward the porch, and called out, "*Der Kessel Mann!*"

It was a kettle salesman and, my, he was a smooth talker! Placing them on the porch bench, he displayed his wares—shiny, gleaming, five-ply solid-core cooking kettles, just what I've been needing for quite some time, because my old set of aluminum cookware is wearing out. I gazed wistfully at the shiny assortment and told the salesman that under no circumstances would I be able to afford them.

Without a word, he sadly (or so I thought) repacked the kettles and carried them back to his car. I thought he might even be upset or angry, but in a few minutes he was back again, displaying a second-hand set on the bench.

"I have just what you need," he said. "Almost as good as new, yet not one-third of the price of a new set. All three-ply stainless steel, and it will last a lifetime. The handles will be replaced free."

The price he quoted me was still too high, I thought, and I firmly resolved I would be satisfied with my old set. But the salesman lowered his price a bit, and when he left, the shiny kettle set was still on the bench. He had either hypnotized or brainwashed me into writing a check.

Even before Kermit came in, the pangs of remorse hit me. What had happened to my good judgement? Why was I so gullible? How could I have been so extravagant?

There was a look of disbelief on Kermit's face when he came in for supper and saw the kettle set. He opened the checkbook and gave a little gasp. I think the look of misery in my eyes prevented him from saying much, but his eyes spoke volumes.

Right after supper Kermit went to his desk and got a postcard and pen, and as soon as he had addressed the postcard and written his message, he went back to work, not taking the time to visit as he usually did. Oh, what pangs of remorse I suffered when I saw that he had written to the harness maker to cancel his order of a new harness for the horse. I know that we very badly need a new harness, because our old one is nearly worn through and mended in several places. Oh, what if it tears while we're on the road and causes an accident?

Aunt Miriam came to visit, but I couldn't share with her.

When Kermit came in at 10:15 last night, I apologized right away and told him how sorry I am. He was very kind about it and said I deserved a new kettle set and I should forget about it. But that made me feel worse than ever. I think the scolding I deserved would have been easier to take.

Soon after breakfast this morning, a car came in the lane. It was Pamela Styer. My despised kettle set was still on the kitchen counter, and Pam admired it, saying it was just what she needed and wondered where I had found such a treasure. Immediately I had a plan, and I turned into a sales lady myself. In just about five minutes Pam was the new owner of the set and was writing out a check for it. I was jubilantly happy and went to retrieve Kermit's postcard from the mailbox. We wouldn't need to cancel the harness order after all! Oh, my, how lighthearted I felt! What a relief to be rid of the despised kettles!

Kermit and I had a long talk tonight. He is so good and kind, and although I knew he readily forgave me for rashly splurging and did not reproach me, I was very happy to tell him that Pam bought the kettle set from me and we would be able to buy the new harness after all. Seeing the expression on his face was worth all the self-berating and remorse I went through.

Neighbor Barbianne walked across the field this evening, bringing a bouquet of blue irises and a scrapbook of hers for me to look at. It is so nice to have friendly neighbors! I found something in her scrapbook that I thought worthy of copying here:

A Marital Alphabet

Accept one another as he or she is.
Be sensitive to each other's needs.
Compliment each other regularly.
Don't go to bed angry or with an argument unsettled.
Express your love and appreciation for each other daily.
Forgive one another totally and unconditionally.
Give 100 percent of yourself to the marriage relationship.
Honor one another.
Identify areas of conflict, and work on root causes.
Judge not.
Keep courting.
Listen to one another.
Measure up to your God-assigned role in the marriage.
Never drag up past mistakes.
Open your hearts to one another in honesty and understanding.
Pray together.
Quit nagging.
Renew your commitment to God and each other.
Speak the truth in love.
Treat each other as friends and lovers.
Undergird one another in child rearing, work, and responsibilities.
View your marriage as a covenant before God.
Worship together.
X-ray your heart with the prayer, "Search me, O God, and know my heart: try me, and know my thoughts; and see if there be any wicked way in me. . ." (Psalm 139:23, 24)
Yield yourselves daily to the will of God.
Zero in on common goals and interests, and enjoy each other for life.

April 28

We have new neighbors, a family by the name of Grant, on the farm just north of us, whose land joins our back fields. Going by way of the road would be at least a mile, but by way of

Forget-Me-Not Lane it isn't far. A big truck was there today bringing their furnishings, and Kermit went to help unload. The place has been unoccupied for five years and looks it, but the Grants have already spruced it up quite a bit and probably will continue to do so.

According to the description of the family that Kermit gave me, the mother recently died, but there is an elderly lady who keeps house for them. There are four children: a thirteen-year-old boy named Jack; twelve-year-old twins named Nick and Nola; and a ten-year-old girl named Ginny. Apparently the children were very friendly and chattered away like old friends, but the father of the family didn't seem inclined to friendliness—he didn't have much to say. Kermit told me the father never once smiled or thanked him for coming to help. I think he must have appreciated it, because they had a lot of possessions and unloading it all was quite a task. I hope we can be good neighbors.

Sadie is planning to pick a bouquet of tulips and to bake a shortcake, and after my foot is better she wants me to go with her to the Grants to deliver them and to meet the housekeeper and the children. Neighbors are rather highly esteemed around here and we want to make the most of the ones we have. We never know how soon we may need their help, and they ours.

Here is another paraphrase of Proverbs 31, one that is slightly different from the one I copied in my last journal.

Proverbs 31

What is the value of an upright man?
He is worth more than a dozen bars of gold.
He treats his wife in loving ways every day,
*   so that she may safely trust in him.*
He works diligently to provide for his family.
He is strong and able from his many hours of labor.
When a man, either a brother or a stranger, is in need,
*   he will not hesitate to give his help.*
He doesn't worry when the winds and rain beat down
*   on his home, for he has built their house on the rock.*
Sincerity and humbleness are some of his many assets.
He speaks with knowledge and understanding and
*   does not provoke anyone to anger.*
His children look to him with respect and his wife
*   humbly submits to him.*

The rich and handsome man is misleading, but the man
who loves the Lord with all his heart is far better.
For he is known by his good deeds and kind spirit
which will last far longer than riches and fame.

April 29

I'm still spending a good bit of time on the swing under the cherry tree. Mr. and Mrs. Robin are so busy building a nest about ten feet above me that they hardly notice my presence. I spent the morning keeping Kermit company in the shop. Next week Jared is coming and we will be really glad for his help. I haven't heard from Treva's mom yet, but I'm hoping she will be coming also.

The midwife paid me a visit today, and she says everything is fine and that I shouldn't be surprised if the newcomer arrives several weeks early. That's fine with me! It seems I've been waiting forever for the event. (Smiles)

This afternoon Mom drove over in the *Dach Vegli* and took me to see Grandpa Dave and Grandma Annie. It seems as if almost everyone in this neighborhood calls them that, even though they never had any children of their own. Annie can still quilt, but she can't walk very well. Dave spends his time cracking shellbarks and pecans and picking out the nut meats. Their minds are still keen, and visiting with them is a pleasure. They still go visiting using their old horse and their *Dach Vegli*.

Grandpa told a rather incredible story that he claims is true—it was told to him by his grandfather and happened in the state of Michigan.

A certain farmer, who had an insufficient quantity of seed corn to plant because of an early frost the previous year, sent an order to a seed company in another state for a supply of ninety-day seed corn. The seeds arrived in due time, and the farmer planted eleven acres of corn. It grew rapidly and became tall and sturdy. But when fall came, he saw that he had been deceived—it was not ninety-day corn at all. When the frosts came, the ears were just beginning to fill out and would not be ready to harvest until long after it could be damaged by frost.

One day when the farmer was walking through the cornfield, he realized that it could not reach maturity. He fell to his knees there in the field and spoke to the Heavenly Father with a prayer similar to this: "Father, I have been deceived in this corn; according to the season and the nature of the corn, it cannot ripen. But, Father, it is all in Thy hands. I have given myself and all I have in Thy care. It is only by Thy power that this field of corn will ever ripen. Thy will be done. I will not complain." While the farmer was speaking to the Lord, a heavenly peace filled his soul.

Frost after frost came, and there was ice as thick as window glass, but the corn did not suffer frost damage. The neighbors were astonished and talked about it among themselves, wondering how this farmer's corn could stay green and growing until it ripened, in spite of so many killing frosts. They had never before, nor since, seen such a crop of corn. The farmer had a firm faith that the Lord would answer the prayers of the faithful in heart, and that no good thing would He withhold from them who walk uprightly, and the farmer was rewarded. A remarkable story.

Grandpa Dave and Grandma Annie are so kindhearted and affectionate towards each other, just like the most devoted bride and groom. Here's part of a poem I found that just suits them:

> *When down the western slope they trudge together;*
> > *When she a crown of silvery white is wearing,*
> *May she, close-clinging to his hand,*
> > *ne'er stop to wonder whether*
> *The old-time love for her he still is bearing.*
> *God grant—He's granted lots of things*
> > *that gladdened them—*
> *His faded lips with kisses she may smother;*
> *That when they've lost the fire of youth*
> > *they twain may be*
> *Two gentle, gray-haired folks*
> > *that love each other.*

May 1

I spent the forenoon helping Kermit in the woodworking shop. I enjoy working with him, and it's good for me to get out of the house for a bit. Then, this afternoon Sadie and I finally took the time to visit the new neighbors. She drove over on her pony cart and we went by way of the road. Sadie had baked a shortcake topped with a delicious-looking glaze, and I brought a pan of butterscotch bars.

Bessie, the housekeeper, met us at the door and welcomed us inside in a friendly manner. She was delighted with the cake and butterscotch bars and invited us to sit down. Bessie is a great-aunt to the children and says she hardly has the energy to do more than cook the meals and do the dishes. She said it was a big change for her to move in with her nephew's family after living alone in a small apartment for over thirty years. Mr. Grant isn't here very often and the children are allowed to freely roam in the neighborhood. The most surprising thing she told us was that Mr. Grant used to be a minister, but when his wife died after suffering from a lengthy illness, he gave up both his profession and his faith. Bessie said that Mr. Grant became remote and bitter, saying that there was no use serving a God who permitted his children to suffer when He had the power to heal.

Kermit and I had a talk about it when I got home, and he said it wasn't right to blame God for the suffering in the world. When His children arrive on that Blessed Shore, God wipes all tears from their eyes and there will be joy forevermore. Kermit said that quite often suffering is either directly or indirectly a result of someone thwarting God's will, because of things that have crept into our universe that were not in God's original plan.

I suppose that now we see "as through a glass darkly," but someday we shall understand. We must remember to pray for Mr. Grant, that he might overcome his bitterness and allow God's love to heal him, and for God to be the burden-bearer. It would be a great pity for Mr. Grant's children to grow up without further Christian teaching and without a church. I think I'll copy a Golden Gem before I head for the garden.

> **Golden Gem for the day:** *Pray daily for faith—it is the gift of God. Trust not in your faith, but trust in the One who gives the faith.*

May 2

Kermit brought in a big bouquet of pink, red, and white tulips tonight from the flowerbed by the garden fence. How thoughtful of him—he knows I like flowers. There are so many out there that cutting some doesn't spoil the beauty of the tulip bed at all. If only we could add some magic potion to the water to make the cut flowers stay nice for a month, or even a few weeks. Sadie did give me a "recipe" to add to the water to make the flowers stay nice longer. I'll see if it makes a difference.

2 teaspoons Realemon
1 teaspoon sugar
1/2 teaspoon Clorox
Add ingredients to one quart of water.
Change the water every day.

Mom came over tonight and brought me the infant sleeper pattern I had requested. She also brought me a clipping that someone had sent her before the birth of her first baby.

Ten Commandments
For a First-Time Mother

1. Thou shalt not forget to thank God who created thy baby. This precious bundle is a gift of love and a miracle, indeed.

2. Thou shalt humble thyself before God and seek His wisdom as thou dost face this new responsibility of caring for a living soul.

3. Thou shalt impress upon thyself that taking time to love and care for baby is not wasted time. As thou dost enjoy thy baby and love him, he'll return thy love.

4. Thou shalt accept the idea that thy housework must slide a bit, for it is a wise mother who recognizes she must rest to renew her strength.

5. Remember that no two babies grow alike. Accept the rate thy baby grows and do not compare him with thy friends' babies.

6. Thou shalt not covet thy neighbor baby's curly hair or four-month tooth or ability to walk at eight months.

7. Thou shalt not fret thyself if thou dost not get anything else done but caring for baby and light housework. Some things may need to be overlooked for awhile. Things will perish, but the soul of thy baby will live forever.

8. Thou shalt adjust thyself to night feedings, for this is a time that as baby snuggles next to thee he will also grow very close to thy heart.

9. Thou shalt not suffer thy husband to feel left out because thy baby needs more attention than he.

10. Thou shalt encourage thy husband to hold and care for baby, for thy baby needs a father's love, too.

Greetings from my hospital room. Kermit brought my journal along when he came to visit tonight. It will give me something to do, for the days get long and lonely here.

It was a week ago today, soon after I had made my last journal entry, that I started not feeling well. I decided to lie down for awhile, hoping I'd feel better after a good rest. But, to my alarm, after my nap I felt worse instead of better. I thought of the journal that Great-grandmother Gertrude has, when Feronica's mother died from hemorrhaging when her baby was born.

Just what is wrong with me? I wondered. It wasn't yet time for the baby to come. If only Mom were here, I kept thinking. I hardly dared to move. I dozed off into a troubled sleep and had a frightening dream—it was about a tiny coffin with a little waxen form in it, like a doll. Suddenly, I awoke with a start. Kermit came in for supper, and in a moment he was bending over me, concern showing on his face.

"What is the matter?" he asked worriedly.

"I wish I knew," I answered, feeling more alarmed by the moment. "I think you'd better ask Pam Styer to call the doctor. He will probably send me to the hospital."

Kermit's face turned pale, and he left immediately to saddle our new horse. In a few minutes I heard hoofbeats thundering in the lane. He was going faster than I ever knew him to go, even when rounding up cattle on our Tall Cedars Homestead.

I felt weak and panicky, and it seemed ages until Kermit was back, telling me that Pam would be over in a few minutes to take me to the emergency room. A new fear gripped me then— going to the emergency room sounded very serious. Kermit packed a bag for me, and gone were my dreams of having a peaceful home delivery with the midwife in attendance. The ride to the hospital seemed long and rather frightening, because I did not know what lay ahead of us.

Oh, dear, I must go. Nurse Mazie was just in, telling me it is time to get some rest. Rest! All I do is rest!

Most of the nurses are very kind to me and I've made a lot of friends in the week I've been in the hospital. I'm on complete bed rest, which means just that—no getting up for anything. Kermit brought some books to read and some writing material—it's a good time for letter writing. I also made a list of more things he is to bring, things I can do in bed, such as crocheting booties, etc.

There has been loneliness, boredom, trying hours, and tears, and I have wished for more patience. My condition is stabilized, but I'm not out of danger yet, so I must stay and try to ward off self-pity. I've been learning more about praying and waiting, for "prayer is a shield to the soul, a sacrifice to God, and a scourge for Satan."

As I wrote in the beginning of this entry, most of the nurses are very kind to me, but there is one whom I shall call Mrs. "C," who apparently has no sympathy for anyone. One of the other nurses told me Mrs. C received nurse's training at a military school and she obeys the rules to the letter, rather than the spirit of the law. She lets herself be heard and has no conscience against raising her voice. If a close relative comes to visit a patient between visiting hours when she is on duty, that is just too bad because they will not get to see the patient, even if they have come cross-country.

Nurse Mazie makes up for her, though; she would do anything to please me and goes the second mile in kindness. She is a Christian and gave me a book of poems to read. I'll copy one here about Hannah, who gave her son to the Lord.

Real Mothers

In agony of prayer he was conceived.
In a white ecstasy a son was born.
She prayed. God gave the answer. She believed.
Her heart that once had been so sorrow torn,
Was lifted up until her praises rang,
Among the songs the white-robed angels sang.

In gratitude to God for answered prayer,
She loaned her son to Him while he should live.

She brought him to the temple, left him there,
The greatest gift a human heart can give.
The little cloaks she made him through the years,
Have touched a million mother hearts to tears.

God, may there be more Hannahs in our day;
More sons conceived in prayer and loaned to Thee
To serve the church, or on the common way,
Bear golden fruitage for eternity.
Unto the temple of Thy holy hill,
May mothers being their sons and daughters still.

While I was copying the poem, I began to think about Hannah of the Bible, and the line in the poem, "may there be more Hannahs in our day." I fell in love with the name Hannah. It's really pretty. Tonight when Kermit comes to visit, I'll see what he thinks about it. We've already chosen a name for a boy but cannot decide on a girl's name. I'm kind of hoping for a girl. Kermit wants a girl, too, but, of course, we'd be thrilled with a boy, too.

May 11

I'm feeling much better! I had lots of visitors tonight besides Kermit—Mom and Pop brought the whole family. Seeing their dear, kind faces gave me a case of *hemveh.* I told them about the run-in I had with Mrs. C, and we laughed together about it. Here is what happened. I awoke early, long before anyone else was stirring, feeling better than I had in a week. In fact, the doctor was in yesterday and said I am past the critical stage and would soon have more privileges.

When I awoke this morning, I felt so well that I longed to take a shower and shampoo my hair. The nurses hadn't washed my hair since I came, and I didn't mention it because I didn't see how it could be done while in bed. My hair is long and thick, reaching below my waist when I have it loose, and it takes a lot of water to shampoo it. A shampoo and shower at the same time would feel wonderful, I thought, with the refreshing water running down through my hair and over me. Would I dare to do it?

I slowly got out of bed and went to the window. The stars were still shining and all was quiet. My roommate was sleeping and all was quiet in the hall. I thought I could take my shower without disturbing anyone. I knew that Mrs. C was on night duty, but she probably was at the desk at the nurse's station—she seldom checked on me anyway.

I couldn't resist. I tiptoed into the shower stall, closed the door quietly, and turned on the water, rubbing shampoo into my hair. Oh, how refreshing all that water felt, cascading down over me. I had just finished rinsing my hair and wrapped it in a towel, when I heard hurried footsteps; the door swung open. There stood Mrs. C!

"Just what do you think you are doing in here?" she yelled, glaring at me.

"J—just taking a shower," I stammered, quaking inwardly and feeling as if I was guilty of a crime.

Mrs. C's face looked like a thundercloud. "Get right back to bed and stay there until the doctor allows you to get up."

She called a nurse to help me get back to bed. It was Nurse Maizie! I was so glad to see her, and as she tucked me back in, she whispered, "I'm sure her shouting did more harm than a shower could have."

Oh, well, I was none the worse for it and it was worth it to feel so refreshingly clean. My hair was dry by the time the breakfast trays came, and I combed and re-rolled it, and pinned it back up.

I sure enjoyed my visitors tonight. Kermit lingered after the others left. He likes the name Hannah, too.

May 12

Very early this morning our little bundle of joy arrived, three weeks early. She weighs nearly six pounds, and we named her Hannah Leigh. Kermit got here just in time for the great event. All seems well—we have so much to be thankful for. I do believe she's going to be a blue-eyed blonde, and her features are just like Kermit's.

> *One tiny crumpled fist lies as she dropped it,*
> *The other I have gathered in my hand—*
> *So fragile, pink, and white, like apple blossoms,*
> *And yet complete. I cannot understand,*
> *This miracle. Though old, it has such strangeness,*

For a new mother who has just been born,
With her first child. My heart is overflowing,
With holy gladness as I watch her form.

Hannah is perfectly and exquisitely formed, and the miracle seems beyond comprehension. It is an awesome and humbling experience. Kermit thinks Hannah is the dearest and sweetest thing he ever saw.

Here we are at home again, and Baby is asleep in her little white bassinet. Sadie brought us our supper, and a delicious one it was! She stayed to wash the dishes and tidy up the kitchen. Kermit did a good job of keeping things in shape around here in the nearly two weeks I was away, but, of course, it needed a woman's touch. He said the place seemed empty without me; there was no one singing around the house, no happy smile to greet him, and the house echoed with silence. There always seemed to be dirty dishes in the sink and crumbs on the floor, and there was never any supper ready when he came in. But he managed, and now we are together again as a family. I hope I'll know how to care for a baby; there is so much to learn.

Here is a poem I got from Mom.

What Would You Take?

What would you take for that soft little head
Pressed close to your face at time for bed,
For that white dimpled hand in your own held tight,
And the dear little eyelids kissed down for the night?
What would you take?

What would you take for that smile in the morn,
Those bright dancing eyes and the face they adorn,
For the sweet little voice that you hear all day
Laughing and cooing, yet nothing to say?
What would you take?

What would you take for those pink little feet,
Those chubby red cheeks and that mouth so sweet,
For the wee tiny fingers and little soft toes,
The wrinkly little neck and that funny little nose?
What would you take?

My parents and family were here tonight and I was a bit miffed when Jethro said, "Why, she's wrinkled and red!"

Kermit told him with a chuckle, "Probably not more wrinkled and red than you were when you were a baby."

Sis wishes she could be my *Maad*, but she knows she's needed at home, and tomorrow the van will come, bringing both our helpers, Jared and Treva.

Mom and Pop presented us with a baby gift, a nice wooden high chair. Will little Hannah ever be big and strong enough to sit in it? I weighed her this afternoon and she hasn't gained an ounce yet. Mom says it's too soon, and babies usually lose some weight at first, so I suppose it's okay.

Baby Hannah is very *brauuv* and spends a lot of time sleeping. Sometimes I can hardly get her awake to nurse.

Here's another baby poem.

The New Baby

"How funny and red!"
That's what they said.
"Why, there's nothing but fuzz
On top of his head."
And they lifted the covers
To look at his feet,
"Oh, how tiny and wrinkled
And red as a beet!"
And I heard them whispering
Behind my back,
"Did you ever think
He would look like that,

All wrinkled and red
Like a baby bird?"
Of course they didn't
Know that I heard.
But I had to smile
When the baby was fed
To see how fast
They lined up by his bed,
And in spite of the fact
He was wrinkled and thin,
They all begged for a turn
At holding him.

Aunt Miriam came this forenoon with a gift of a dozen diapers. Soon after she left, the Grant youngsters came skipping down Forget-Me-Not Lane with a batch of brownies Nola had made all by herself. The children said Aunt Bessie sent her love. They are very nice, well-mannered children, and I didn't mind that they wanted to hold Hannah. She didn't even wake up, she just yawned and stretched and flailed her little fists for a minute before dropping off again.

This afternoon the van arrived, bringing Treva and Jared, our Maad and Gnecht. Treva was satisfyingly enamored over the baby, oohing and aahing, and exclaiming how cute and sweet she is. Jared went right to the shop. He has some experience in woodworking and is just who Kermit needs.

I'm feeling weary today, for Hannah seemed to have a bellyache last night, and Kermit took his turn walking the floor with her. I'm glad Treva's here to help, in case it happens again.

May 17, Sunday

I took a short walk down Forget-Me-Not Lane, the first in about three weeks, and was newly enraptured by the beauties of spring. I look forward to taking Hannah along on my strolls. The wild cherry tree by the creek was in blossom, and the morning breeze was indescribably fragrant. The water glided peacefully over the rocks, and the birds sang sweetly from the trees. I brought my Bible with me; it was such a lovely, peaceful place to have my devotions. It will be quite awhile before I can attend church services again—it seems quite awhile since I've been there.

We had visitors this afternoon. Rudy and Barbianne walked over to see the baby. We had a nice visit; they are still the same good-natured couple they always were.

The supper dishes are done and Kermit is sitting on the Boston rocker while holding Hannah, trying to get her to smile. I told him she is too young for smiles, but I suppose he thinks that because she is ours, she will be a super-baby and he keeps trying. I think that seeing them together like that is the prettiest picture I've ever seen.

He Chose Me!

God had a baby all planned out
For someone down here below,
From the silky floss on the little head,
To the tip of a wee, pink toe.

A tiny nose and two big, blue eyes,
And a wisp of a baby chin,
Dimpled hands, rosebud mouth, and two tiny feet,
All ready some heart to win.

And God looked down on the earth below
Trying a mother to see,
And of all those women with outstretched arms,
Just think! He picked me!

As I felt that little heart beat 'gainst my own,
Down I went on my bended knee,
And I thanked that wonderful God above,
For seeing and choosing me.

And every day as the hours pass by
And new dimples and smiles I see,
I wonder how God in His infinite grace
Ever happened to pick out me.

I feel my heart full of thankful words,
But somehow I can't express
The thankfulness I really feel
In possessing a treasure like this.

So in order to thank the Father above,
The best way would seem to be
To teach our baby to return the love
God felt when He picked out me.

May 18

Two baby cards and letters came in the mail today—
one from Kermit's mom, and one from Rachel and Ben, express-
ing their congratulations and rejoicing with us. They came at an
appropriate time, just when I needed a lift. I believe I have the
"baby blues." It started last night when I was feeling extra
weary because Hannah was so fussy. I suddenly felt drained of
all energy and longed to climb into bed and sleep blissfully,
without a care in the world, until I woke up feeling refreshed
and energetic.

But Hannah was yelling, and when I picked her up and
tried to feed her, she refused to cooperate. She only screamed

louder, waving her little fists. Treva was out mowing the grass, and Kermit was busy in the shop, so I walked the floor with the crying baby, my own tears also falling. It was then that I heard a knock on the door, and Aunt Miriam stepped inside.

What a relief to let her take over for awhile, but to my embarrassment, after she offered a few sympathetic words a floodgate of tears let loose. Of course, Aunt Miriam was very concerned, but to my bewilderment, the more she expressed her sympathy, the faster the tears flowed. At first she seemed worried, but then she calmly told me this was a common phenomenon when new mothers were overly tired.

I was soon smiling again, and Hannah had calmed enough to nurse. My, what an upheaval such a fragile bundle can make!

Then we had a bumpy night. First of all, Hannah didn't settle down until 11:30 p.m, then an hour later she was crying again. I was too sleepy to get up right away, then discovered she was choking on mucous! After that, I hardly dared fall asleep for fear it would happen again. It seemed as if I was up and down every hour or so. Finally at 4:00 a.m., I let Kermit have a turn and was able to get a few hours of solid sleep. Yes, having a baby in the house is still *wunderbaar* (sometimes).

Today I seem to be suffering from extreme weariness, even though I had a few good naps. But Hannah is worth every tired bone and every hour of lost sleep.

I'll copy the "Beatitudes For Mothers" I got out of Barbianne's scrapbook.

Beatitudes For Mothers

Blessed is the mother who takes time to rock and cuddle her baby; for the mother who does not, will someday wish she had!

Blessed is the mother who will exclaim over every bouquet of wilted dandelions her little one brings and put them in a vase on the table! For she is teaching courtesy and the graciousness of giving and receiving.

Blessed is the mother who has the grace to listen, really listen, to her talkative four-year-old; for this is one important link in the chain of teaching respect.

Blessed is the mother who does not remake the bed her five-year-old has made (at least not while he is watching).

Blessed is the mother who will accept with thanks every picture that her first grader has drawn for her and will hang them on the walls, even though company is coming.

Blessed *is the mother who can remind her son seven times a day to hang up his coat and cap, without giving up and doing it for herself; for patience will eventually be rewarded.*

Blessed *is the mother who means "no" when she says "no" and cannot be moved by tears, screams, threats, or persistent argument. Also blessed is the mother who sees to it that her child completes each task that she has assigned to him, for she is preparing him to be a person of character.*

Blessed *is the mother who reads good stories to her children, especially Bible stories, for she is giving them a priceless treasure.*

Blessed *is the mother who does not laugh at her little one when he haltingly tells her his worries, problems, or fears; for then that child will still come to her for advice when he is a teenager.*

Blessed *is the mother who purposes never to talk about other people's shortcomings in front of her children: whether it be the faults of her husband, the ministers, church members, or their own brothers and sisters. Blessed too is the mother who does not yield to the temptation to say to her child, "Why can't you be good like your brother?"*

Blessed *is the mother whose children know that she reads her Bible and prays by herself. Likewise blessed are the children who can see that their mother truly cares about pleasing God; for they are receiving an example more valuable than a hundred sermons heard with the ear.*

Blessed *is this mother, for she shall rejoice in the time to come; her children will rise up and call her blessed.*

Part Two

Neighborhood Frolics

We received a letter today from our little "happy campers," Chet, Diane, and Billy, who lived in the range shelter on the island in our meadow last summer at Beechwood Acres. The letter was really from the children's aunt, and the children had made greeting cards. Their stepfather is not well again, and the children were supposed to stay with their aunt this summer in Georgia, but due to unforeseen circumstances, that won't be possible. Their aunt wondered if the children could stay with us until fall.

I sighed a bit ruefully when I thought about it—I am hardly up to coping with the care of a baby, much less three additional boarders. But, of course, my strength should be returning after awhile, then maybe things will look a bit different.

Tonight was such a calm, lovely evening that I sat out on the porch swing under the cherry tree with Baby Hannah, enjoying the peace and serenity of the evening. What a joy to see Sadie making her way down the lane, coming across the stepping stones in the creek, and heading our way. When I told her about our letter, after reading it herself, she had the wonderful idea of having the three children stay with them this summer. She is going to talk with Aunt Miriam and Uncle Nate about it, and then let us know. That would suit me just fine, but it's for them to decide.

Of course, the children's aunt had no idea that we have a newborn in our home or she wouldn't have requested what she did, but perhaps things will work out for them to come anyway.

Kermit joined me on the swing after he finished in the shop for the day. He still hasn't gotten a smile from Hannah, but he keeps trying. We had a heart-to-heart talk then. I cherish those golden moments of togetherness. The sunset was glorious, somehow reminding us of God's plan of salvation. The shed blood of Jesus can wash away our sins and make our souls sparkling white. His love sustains us, a love so deep and marvelous that He was willing to go through the agony of Gethsemane to bring it to us, the fullness of joy in His presence, the grace that is sufficient for His children, and the peace which passeth all understanding.

Kermit feels as though the woodworking business is slowly "getting off the ground," as he worded it, and hopefully we can soon lessen our debt load.

May 20

Treva is a good *Maad* and loves to cook, bake, and even do dishes. As soon as the work inside is done, she goes out to help in the woodworking shop; she is there now.

Hannah is in her new little infant seat, her blue eyes open wide, their glance already wonderingly following me. I dream of the time when she will gurgle and coo in baby language, smile dazzling smiles, hold a toy in her hand, and reach out for me. I didn't know babies could be so sweet and took so much care. Mom gave me a pair of baby shoes that I used to wear. They were scuffed and worn, but plated in bronze, with a nice inscription on the base. I'll save Hannah's first shoes, too, and give them to her someday. Mom gave me a poem to go with the shoes.

Baby's Shoes

Two worn little shoes
With a hole in the toe;
Why have I saved them?
Well, all mothers know
There's nothing so sweet
As a baby's worn shoes
And the patter of footsteps
Following you.

The feet they once held
Have grown slender and strong;
Tonight they'll be tired
From working so long.
I guided her feet
When she wore such as these;
Dear God, may I ask Thee,
To guide them now, please.

June 1

Sadie didn't let any grass grow under her feet after Aunt Miriam and Uncle Nate gave their consent to take Chet, Billy, and Diane this summer, and they have already arrived. They all came to see us tonight. Their aunt was along, and she will leave for home tomorrow morning. The children were excited about their plane ride.

Diane loves Baby Hannah and says she wants to come over every day. While they were here, the Grant youngsters came over, and the two sets of children hit it off right away and were soon playing a game of ball tag as if they were old friends. After awhile the boys wandered down to the creek, and very soon they came running back, with Jack holding an ugly-looking scrap of life in his hands. It was a baby crow they had found under a tree; it must have fallen out of its nest. It was screeching at the top of its lungs. My inclination would have been to put it back into the nest if possible. But oh, no, the boys wanted to raise it for their pet. They soaked bread crumbs in milk and popped it piece by piece into the wide-open mouth. The bird gulped it down as fast as it could swallow and was soon clamoring for more. The baby crow can't help but thrive on all the attention it gets, for the boys were busy catching bugs and flies. They even got the girls interested, too. The question is, where will they keep the bird? They finally decided to leave it here where Jared and Treva can watch over it.

The produce that Kermit raised is looking good, because we had just the right amount of rainfall in May. We should have a lot of helpers if we put all the neighborhood youngsters to work.

After our visitors had left, I put Hannah into her infant seat and sat out on the porch capping the strawberries Treva had picked. Mmmmm! Luscious. My mouth waters for homemade strawberry ice cream. The floribunda roses on the big bush beside the back walk will soon be blooming. June is a lovely month indeed! I'll miss the fragrance of freshly mown hay this year, for we do not have any. Oh, well, maybe the fragrance will drift across the field from Rudy's place.

Hannah's getting *grittlich*, so I'd better go.

June 16

Baby Hannah is five weeks old today and is doing well. She only awakens once during the night anymore, then after her feeding she goes right back to sleep. What a blessing! She weighs over ten pounds and is getting more dimpled all the time!

As for our little pet crow, he too is growing and doing well. He is already sprouting feathers and seems to constantly have its mouth wide open, waiting for someone to pop in some bread soaked in milk, bugs, or flies. He hops around outside, following whomever is willing to pay him any attention. He loves to hide in the garden under the green leaves in the bean row, or under the flowers in the pansy bed.

Chet, Diane, and Billy are over here a lot, and when they are tussling on the lawn, the bird joins in the fun—he's already inclined to mischief. If they're not careful, he will even pull their hair or tweak ears. No one ever really picked out a name for him, but Treva and Jared call it *Groplie*, which means "little crow" in Dutch. The others began to call him Groplie, too, and I suppose Groplie he will stay. I hope we won't regret allowing the boys to keep him; I've heard it said that pet crows can be a nuisance.

The Grant children are back and forth constantly and have also taken a keen interest in the little crow. Kermit has decided that it's getting to be too much, and if they come too often, we'll put them to work. That way they won't keep Jared and Treva from their work. If the children don't like it, they will probably stay home.

Jack has a hankering to learn to drive the horses, but neither he nor Nick like to do any hoeing in the field. I suppose that's quite natural for boys their age. Nola, Ginny, and Diane are all about the same size, although not really close in age. I had them picking peas today, and they did surprisingly well.

Kermit has succeeded in getting Hannah to smile; next he will have her laughing out loud. Here's a fitting verse:

> *A sweet little baby found its way*
> *Into our home one blessed day.*
> *The father's eye, with joy and love*
> *Beams as he holds this gift from above.*

July 3

We went berrying today and came home with buckets of the blue-black gems to make into jam, pies, and jelly. Sadie had packed a huge hamper full of soup, salad, sandwiches, fruit, and cookies for a real picnic in the woods. Kermit had just hitched the

two big workhorses to the open wagon and Chet, Diane, and Billy were piling on, when Nola and Ginny Grant appeared, wanting to borrow five pounds of sugar. When they heard that we were going berrying and having a picnic, they wanted to go along, and Kermit said they could. They dashed home to ask permission of their dad, and when they came back, Jack and Nick were along, too. They all happily scrambled onto the back of the wagon and seemed to enjoy the day immensely.

You can tell the children have been taught obedience and respect for their elders, but they are full of life and mischief. Kermit has a way of bringing out the best in youngsters, so things were kept under control. For awhile, though, I wasn't so sure. We were all peacefully picking berries when the air was rent with a series of high-pitched shrieks, and Diane went tearing off through the woods as if she was being pursued. Jack rolled on the ground, laughing as hard as he could. He had dropped a fuzzy caterpillar down the back of her dress.

Soon there was another tiff—Nick's half-filled bucket of berries was accidentally knocked over and he blamed Chet for bumping into it, which Chet stoutly denied. Soon voices were raised and fists were flying, but Ginny quickly offered to let Nick have her bucketful, then got on her hands and knees and scooped up the spilled berries with cupped hands (blessed are the peacemakers). Peace and order was soon restored and the tiff forgotten.

It was such a gorgeous day, with skies of clear blue and the woods so green, and the birds twittering in the brush. We ate our lunch beside the clear, rippling creek. The water was so clear that we could see the stones on the bottom, the little minnows darting around, and sometimes even a crab quickly disappearing beneath a rock. It was all so peaceful and I think I dozed off for awhile.

I was awakened by the cry of, "Where's Billy?"

I sprang up in alarm. We searched frantically, peeking behind every rock and fallen log, beating the bushes and calling for Billy. Finally, we spread out to search; Sadie found him curled up in a ball on a bed of leaves with a chubby arm under his rosy cheeks nearly hidden by his straw hat, which had fallen forward. Sadie snatched him up with a glad cry and carried him back to the wagon, much to our relief.

By mid-afternoon, we were all too warm and tired and quite ready to start for home. The boys wanted to take a quick dip in the creek before we left, and when the girls saw them, of course they wanted to do the same. Kermit found a suitable spot for them further down the creek and around a bend.

This evening we were busy canning berries, and Nola and Ginny stayed to help. Sadie had a new recipe for jam that she wanted to try. Treva helped, too, and at last the kitchen is clean again. I think I'll join the family out on the lawn to watch the stars come out. Kermit and the boys just came in from working in the produce field. Baby Hannah did surprisingly well on her first picnic.

July 22

It seems as if Billy, Chet, and Diane are here as much as at Sadie's, and sometimes they sleep here, too, which they did tonight. Billy gave me a scare. I had filled the foot tub with warm water for their nightly foot washing before bed and set it out beside the porch steps. Billy chose to be first, and I noticed that he reached into the flower bed and picked up something from underneath the petunias, but I didn't give it a second thought. After I heard Diane say her bedtime prayer, said goodnight, and tucked her into bed, I went into Billy's room to tuck him in and say goodnight. I thought he had a rather guilty look in his blue eyes, and when an ugly-looking toad hopped out from under the sheet, I knew why! He's a great one for collecting things such as bugs, interesting stones and leaves, snails, etc. Maybe he has the makings of a budding biologist.

I told Billy that the toad liked his freedom as much as Billy did, and that the best place for the toad would be in the garden where he can catch the bugs that bother our growing vegetables. So he gingerly carried it outside and nestled it carefully underneath a cabbage leaf. When he again came upstairs, he was carrying Groplie on his shoulder and begged for the bird to be allowed to sleep in his room. I vetoed that idea, too, and when Billy begged for another bedtime story, I couldn't say no again. He fell asleep before the story was finished, with his blonde curls tumbling over his forehead and a smile on his face. He is a dear little boy, and I wish I could shield him from the trials and temptations that he might have to face in his life.

Baby Hannah seems to grow sweeter and more lovable every day, if such a thing is possible. She gets plenty of attention when the girls are here—sometimes more holding than is good for her; I hope we don't spoil her. They brush her hair into a curl on the top of her head (a "kcwpic" curl).

Here is a poem I liked:

They say that mothers have no pay,
But Daughter smiled at me today,
And Sonny stopped and hugged me tight
As I went in to say good-night.

Dear God, please help me on my way,
To be more faithful every day,
And thank You for the shining gold
I have as these small lives I mold.

July 23

Nola and Ginny came today, carrying a box of goodies. They asked if they could make a cake here for Bessie, their housekeeper, because tomorrow is her birthday. They also had the ingredients for their dad's favorite brownie recipe. They wanted to have a party in the evening to surprise both of them. Of course, we said they could. The box contained a cake mix, confectioner's sugar, cream cheese, nuts, chocolate chips, and a brownie mix. Kermit and the boys had planned to spend the afternoon working in the field, and I had plans to drive to Mom's with a pattern she had asked to borrow, and to pick up the four bushels of peaches we had ordered. The girls had the kitchen to themselves.

The cake mix was easy enough to prepare, and while Ginny and Nola stirred that, Diane prepared the brownie mix which was supposed to be extra-special and made with great care, the goodies lovingly added. They had great fun singing and stirring, stirring and singing, as they later told me. While their creations were baking in the gas oven, they sat on the couch and told stories. When the baking was finished, they put the cake on a wire rack to cool before they frosted it, and they cut the rich, chewy brownies into squares and stacked them on a platter to cool before they wrapped them. The girls set them on the window-sill to catch the breeze for faster cooling, then went happily out to the blueberry patch to pick blueberries to make a sauce for the cake.

No one thought of taking a drink out to Kermit and the boys, so by mid-afternoon they were thirsty and the boys came trooping in for water. Coming around the corner of the wash house, Nick spied the steaming, freshly-baked bars on the windowsill, and, quickly motioning the others to silence, he sneaked toward the goodies. After all, he and the boys surely deserved at least one brownie apiece after working so hard. Now, if he could only get hold of the platter before the girls saw him! If he had only known that the girls were on the other side of the house and orchard picking blueberries, he wouldn't have been so stealthy about it.

Nick cautiously grabbed the platter of brownies and began to run. While hurrying back to the other boys, his foot hit the edge of the walk and he fell, sprawling on the grass. The platter of brownies flew out of his hand and landed in the flowerbed where stones were arranged around petunias planted in mushroom soil. Sadly disappointed, the boys began to gather up the ruined pieces, and when Jack suggested that they use their pocketknives to cut off the dirty outer edges and eat the centers, they eagerly did so, with the dirty pieces going to Groplie.

When Kermit came in from the field to see what happened to his helpers, there was nothing left to do but confess. Kermit quite sternly told the boys that they should never treat the ladies that way. For punishment, they would have to forfeit their evening of swimming and the girls would go two days in a row. (They have to take turns, because we don't allow them to swim together.) Kermit then told the boys to wash their hands and roll up their sleeves—they would have to help make something to replace the brownies. He got out honey, butter, and sugar, and told the boys they would get a lesson on taffy making (I guess he remembered how to do it from taffy parties in his *rumshpringing* days).

When I walked into the kitchen, it was full of guys merrily pulling long strands of taffy from hand to hand while the girls sat on the sofa watching in amusement. It turned out to be a real party for us, too, and the girls were quite happy with their extra swimming time. How nice of Kermit to take the time off from work to happily save the situation. Maybe next time we go to the grocery store we can get more nuts, cream cheese, and whatever it takes to make good brownies and invite Mr. Grant, Bessie, and the children over for a meal.

We've set up a roadside stand to earn a little money by selling melons and vegetables at retail prices. It will keep us busy, but Sadie will help us out if we get into a pinch. Kermit went to talk with the owner of this little farmette, who has agreed to let us rent it for five years before he sells it. If we work hard, it should give us a chance to make a living, but it will be hard if we ever expect to do anything besides rent. I guess we will have to be even more frugal and thrifty. Maybe in winter I can make quilts to sell or do baking for market.

We visited my parents this evening and told them of our plans. They were very supportive and assured us that as long as they have something to eat, so will we. It is a good feeling to know that we won't have to move right away, and to be assured that there are lots of worse things than having a hard time financially.

On the way back we stopped in at Uncle Nate's and they too offered their help and support. Aunt Miriam went to the attic and brought down an old book she had bought at a neighbor's sale years ago. The cover of the book is missing, and she couldn't think of the title, but it is a story of someone who was trying to make a living on a five-acre piece of land. They were honest, God-fearing people, and it will be interesting to read about how they survived and what hardships they endured. The good part is that it is true, which is much more interesting than fiction. I hope I will get a chance to read it before too long.

July 28

Today we'll have a busy day canning Early Harvest applesauce, and Mom is coming to help, so I will only take the time to copy a poem.

A Mother's Mission

A mother's job is special
And carries strong demands.
With the molding of the little life
God places in her hands.

Though her life may not be glamorous,
The world will see her worth.
For 'tis true "The hands that rock the cradle
Are the hands that rule the earth."

To bring her children up in Christ,
Indeed is very much.
For the years will show her value
By the lives, their lives, will touch.

July 29

There is trouble in our "idyllic" setting. When Rudy and Barbianne were here, Billy took an instant liking to Rudy, and vice versa. Rudy sat him on his knee, and Billy chattered away happily about his collection of bugs and butterflies and rocks. Before they left, Billy came running with a gift for Rudy—a jar containing a twig and a cocoon. Billy told Rudy that soon a lovely butterfly would hatch. If Rudy wasn't delighted, he sure hid it for Billy's sake, and pretended it was one of the best presents he ever received. Rudy dug into his pocket and pulled out five gold-colored coins and gave them to Billy.

After Rudy left, we discovered that the coins were the new dollar coins that were just released and aren't much bigger than a quarter. Billy has been happily playing with them off and on ever since, taking the coins out of his penny bank and laying them down in a row to admire them.

Today the four Grant children were here all day helping to gather produce for the market stand. When dinner was ready, Billy showed the contents of his penny bank, the five golden coins, to Jack and Nick. He laid them in a row on the arm of our little rocker for the boys to admire. Since we were all seated at the table and waiting for them, Billy just left the coins there while we ate, intending to put them back into his bank right after dinner.

As soon as we had raised our heads after giving thanks after the meal, a carriage came driving in the lane. It was Grandma Annie and Grandpa Dave. Kermit and the boys went to help them unhitch while the girls and I made a quick inventory of leftovers. If we had known they were coming, we would have waited to eat. We quickly peeled more potatoes and fried a few more slices of ham, and Treva ran out to the garden for more sweet corn and a head of cabbage for slaw.

The boys came back in with Kermit and Grandpa and sat on the couch while Grandpa and Grandma ate their dinner, not wanting to miss any of the visit. Grandma was as kind and gracious as always, and Grandpa's congenial conversation charmed the Grant children. It wasn't until they were done eating that Billy thought of his gold coins.

Diane was rocking away on her little rocker and the empty bank was on the floor beside her. Billy sprang up from his perch on the footstool, crying, "Oh, my, Diane, are you sitting on my pennies? Get up, *dopper, dopper*!"

Diane denied sitting on the coins, but she did get up, and there were no gold coins to be found. A quick search was made— under the settee, couch, stove, and rocker, but the coins seemed to have disappeared into thin air. Billy was in tears, declaring that someone had stolen his pennies. Kermit reassured him they were bound to turn up somewhere, and that after Grandpa and Grandma left, they would all help to search some more.

After they left, Billy again started howling again, and a more thorough search was made. Finally, Kermit ordered all the boys to sit in a row on the settee, and he asked them individually if they knew what had happened to the coins.

They all stoutly denied it, but did I just imagine it, or did Nick's voice tremble a bit when he answered Kermit, "No, I do not?"

I don't want to blame anyone who is innocent, but just last week Nick sneaked into our pantry and stuffed his pockets full of cookies. When he went home, his dad discovered the bulges and made Nick come back to confess and apologize. I suppose you would call that stealing, for they say that eating while at someone's house isn't stealing, but if you take something from their home and keep it, it is stealing. I hope Nick will be proven innocent, but I guess time will tell, because if he did take the coins, I am sure his sins will find him out. The poor, motherless boy!

There was a heavy thunderstorm this evening, and now the earth is washed clean and sparkling again. The sun came out behind a cloud afterward and a brilliant rainbow of multi-colored hues appeared in the east, a reminder of God's promises.

It was a beautiful day today, and in the evening we all sat out on the lawn watching the stars come out. Groplie hopped around being mischievous, while Diane and Billy tried to teach him to say words, but all he did was squawk. We were reminiscing about our days in Montana and talking of all the good memories we have of the friends we left behind.

Treva and I had a busy day catching up on all the work that had piled up, and she also tended the produce stand. Just before supper, she came running wildly into the house in such agitation that at first she could hardly talk. Her hair had come undone and she was clutching at it with one hand. A thief had cleaned out the money box right before her eyes and in broad daylight, too, and had made off with over a hundred dollars! It wasn't just produce that had been sold; she had also sold homemade bread, shoo-fly pies, homemade noodles, and cookies.

It is certainly not the first time that has happened in this area, but, *Ach my*, how we needed that money! *Ya well,* it's gone now, with very little hope of its recovery. At least it taught us to take more precautions. If only Treva had been able to get the thief's license number. Until now, our customers have been entirely trustworthy and it makes me sad to think about the thief's greed and dishonesty. I hope he will repent and bring the money back sometime.

Hannah is now at a delightful age to hold, and Kermit gets her to laugh out loud. I'll soon be able to put her into her walker.

A Mother's Recreation

Some folks prefer a mountain camp,
Some choose a quiet lake;
Others require a gay resort,
Vacation days to take.
Give me a friendly little woods,
A gently bubbling spring,
A winding brook that ripples by,
While happy bird songs ring.
A little child to skip along,

Or, trusting, hold my hand,
Whose eyes and ears and heart respond
To wonders God has planned.
A mossy log where we may rest,
An hour to meditate.
This is a vacation setting that
I classify first rate.

Golden Gem for today: *The prayer of faith is the joining of the heart, mind, and soul to God, the channel through which we receive all that He has for us.*

August 11

We had a refreshing rain shower tonight, followed by a brilliant rainbow, and it appeared as if one end of it shone right into the orchard.

Billy asked, "Is it true that there is a pot of gold at the end of the rainbow? Ginny told me that."

Diane hooted at his ignorance and set him straight in short order.

Treva said, "I wish it was true—but not a pot of gold, just lots of excitement and adventures."

Kermit said that what we need is a pot of serenity and contentment, or, rather, bushels of it! Treva admitted that Kermit was right; she finds it hard to be content at times and to give herself up in *Gelassenheit.*

We have found out that there have been more robberies in the neighborhood—at the Watsons' some antiques and shop tools stored in the barn were taken, and at their next door neighbor's there were two bicycles stolen. Mr. Watson stopped in a few nights ago to tell us and said we had better be careful; we are probably next on the list. We told him we were already victims at the roadside stand, but Mr. Watson told us it might not be the same robbers.

Jack Grant heard about it and last evening he and Jared decided to prepare for the thieves. They figured that since the most valuable tools and equipment were in the woodworking shop, the thieves would prowl until they found them. There is a rusty iron bell on top of the shop which I suppose was used in earlier days to call workers to the noon meal. They rigged the rope of this bell with pulleys so that it would ring when the door was opened. They also put a bucket of water on the shelf above the same door, attached it to the same rope, and when the door opened, the bucket would spill its contents on the one entering the room.

In case the thieves entered by way of the back door, Jared and Jack put the big galvanized cattle water trough at the bottom of the steps and filled it with water, hoping that the thieves would not see it in the dark and fall into it. They did this last evening without telling anyone else. I guess they figured Kermit wouldn't approve. The final rigging was done just before bedtime.

Jack spent the night here with Jared, hoping the thieves would come. Sometime around midnight, Treva got up to go to the bathroom and heard a creaking sound, as if someone was slowly and stealthily sneaking up or down the stairs.

She waited quietly, hardly daring to breathe, and when she heard the outside kitchen door opening and closing quietly, she suddenly hollered, *"Dieb, dieb!"* (thieves, thieves!) as loud as she could.

Just beneath Treva's open bedroom window were Jared and Jack, sneaking out towards the shop. They had awakened at midnight and decided to check on things outside, hoping to witness the thieves being outwitted. Treva had heard the boys leaving and thought they were burglars. When the boys heard Treva yelling, their first thought was that she must have seen burglars out near the shop.

Without thinking of the consequences, Jared excitedly whispered to Jack, "You go the back way, and I'll go the front way, and we can catch them in the act!"

A few minutes later, Kermit and I heard the bell ring and he was dressed and out the door in a flash. He took the time to light a lantern, and in the shop he found two dripping wet boys, one of them having fallen into the water trough and the other one having been doused with a bucket of water—no burglars in sight!

They were a pair of very sheepish, chastened boys and each grabbed a towel and headed for their bedrooms. The good news is that the police were cruising the neighborhood because Mr. Watson had called them, and they caught the crooks stealing an air compressor at Emanuel's. All's well that ends well.

August 12

Billy sheds tears every day over his lost "pennies," and I wonder if Nick is the one who stole them, for he hasn't come back since the day the coins disappeared, even though the other three Grant children have been back and forth every day. How I wish Nick would confess and return them and be at peace; that is, if he really did steal them. I think he knows that we suspect him and that is why he stays away. If he would make a clean breast of it, we would gladly forgive and forget it.

Rudy stopped in today, and at once Billy told him of the lost coins. Kindhearted Rudy, without hesitating, reached into his pocket and pulled out five more coins exactly like the others, and gave them to Billy. He was such a happy boy!

Sadie, or rather, Uncle Nate and Aunt Miriam, received a letter from the children's aunt in Georgia. Their aunt asked if the children could stay for the upcoming school term. We all have grown quite fond of them, and Sadie made a phone call to Georgia right away with their affirmative answer. The plans now are for Sadie to home-school them. She has her GED and I know she'll make a good teacher. In fact, I hope she will still be available to teach when Hannah turns six. The children were wildly happy, and Billy made the remark that this is as good as a pot of gold at the end of a rainbow.

Here is a poem that I liked about a mother's love and rainbows.

> *What is the secret of a rainbow's charm?*
> *Its silent beauty after wind and storm?*
> *Its multicolored rays above a farm?*
> *Its curve, its arch, and evanescent form?*
>
> *How does a rainbow make my soul expand?*
> *What does its tranquil brilliance fully mean?*
> *The rainbow's hues have helped me understand*
> *Its deeper charm is in the part unseen.*
>
> *What is the secret of a mother's love?*
> *A sense of duty to a helpless one?*
> *A seed of kindness planted from above?*
> *An inner joy and peace for work well done?*
>
> *How does a mother fill the needs she must?*
> *How can she scrub her universe so clean?*
> *The angels know how she fulfills her trust—*
> *Her deeper charm is in her work unseen.*

Hannah is still in her infant seat, cooing in baby language. She's ready for her bath—she dearly loves splashing in the water!

Golden Gem for today: *Dwell not on the difficulties and perplexities of the way. Instead, keep your eyes on the goal, on the glories and beauties of the summit of achievement.*

August 21

The mystery of Billy's missing coins has been solved at last. This evening Treva and Diane were out in the garden picking lima beans, and I was weeding the flower beds nearby when Diane gave a whoop of delight. She had found a little pile of gold coins under the lima bean leaves! Groplie was taking a dust bath nearby, and when he saw her, he hurried over and frantically began to peck at her bare toes. She jumped aside, and in her haste to get away, dropped the coins. Groplie quickly picked up one in his beak and hurried away with it. Diane rescued the rest of the coins while Treva chased Groplie and retrieved the coin from his beak.

All this while I had been secretly blaming Nick for stealing the coins, and he was entirely innocent; Groplie was the guilty culprit. Billy ought to be a happy little boy now with ten coins instead of five, but we persuaded him to share them with the others.

Billy was very happy and sat on the little rocker, singing one song after another that Sadie had taught him: "Mary Had a Little Lamb," "Jesus Loves Me," "This Little Light of Mine," and "*Shlof, Bubly, Shlof.*"

Later in the evening Jack, Nola, Nick, and Ginny came over, and we were happy to tell them that Billy's coins had been found. As a punishment for Groplie, Jack pulled a feather out of his tail and made him squawk, and Groplie ran indignantly to hide under the pumpkin vines in the garden. He sulked and stayed hidden all evening until the Grants went home.

Treva is excited about the dress she is planning to make. I gave her some material, a piece of royal blue softique knit. She is eagerly awaiting a rainy day, or when there is less outside work so she can have a chance to sit at the sewing machine. Her cheery songs fill the house. She and Jared are staying for the winter; they will attend three-hour school here. It is nice to see her so happy.

Sadie came over tonight and helped shell lima beans. Many hands make light work, and everyone took turns telling stories. It is hard to believe that the summer sped by so fast and school will be starting again the week after next. It is nice that the children will be having Sadie for their teacher. I can't imagine what it would have been like having a nice teacher like her.

Treva brought in a bouquet of lovely marigolds and zinnias; they really give the kitchen a splash of color. Autumn is coming, and I am looking forward to it—cooler weather, colorful leaves, cider, pumpkin pie, and wild geese winging their way overhead. Treva and I have finished canning tomatoes—200 quarts in the form of juice, pizza sauce, and ketchup. We sold a lot, too.

Looking out the window, I see Billy giving Groplie a ride in the little wheelbarrow. Oops! He doesn't like it and flew off squawking indignantly, hiding in the petunia bed.

Kermit and Jared are busy in the woodworking shop. Business is still picking up; there are a lot of orders coming in.

Time to go. Hannah is calling me and she won't take "wait awhile" for an answer.

Hannah and I spent the day sitting with little Billy at the hospital. Three days ago he was "flying" down Forget-Me-Not Lane on the scooter and somehow or other managed to hit a fence post. No one saw it happen, but Uncle Nate heard him yelling and came on the run. He is not seriously hurt, but has a bruised liver, and if it should start to bleed, it could be serious.

Billy is allowed to move around carefully, and we spent some time in the hospital playroom this afternoon. It sure is equipped with all kinds of fun things to do: toys of all sorts from blocks and wagons to electronic gadgets and games. There is a big easel with brushes and watercolor paints; puzzles; costumes; hats for dressing up; a big, fully furnished doll house; toy trucks and a fire engine with flashing lights; a railroad set; and shelves of children's books. I believe Billy thought it was an enchanting fairyland, but soon it was time for more blood work, something Billy really dreads.

The doctor and nurses were very kind, taking the time to explain the procedures to him. Billy has no fear of them, and his lack of shyness seems to endear him to them. I'm so glad he's well on the way to recovery.

The hospital brought back a lot of memories. I'm glad that's all in the past and we now have our little Hannah. Here's a poem about mother love.

Mother Love

Whene'er I pause and gaze awhile
Upon my darling, sleeping child,
No words can tell just how I feel,
But mother love is strong and real.

September 7

Billy has returned to Uncle Nate's and already the friends and neighbors have gotten together a sunshine box for him. Packages are starting to arrive, but he is only allowed to open one package a day. My, how exciting it is for him! He opened his first package this morning—he chose the biggest one. It happened to be from Jethro and contained a set of wooden handcrafted horses hitched to a wagon, and a new straw hat.

It seems as if I spent the entire day cooking, because when the Grant children are here and Chet, Diane, Jared, and Treva also, it takes a lot of food. They are still growing and have healthy appetites. It sure is a blessing when they are well and active, rosy-cheeked and suntanned. It makes us appreciate good health more since Billy was in the hospital.

When the busy summer season is over, Treva and I want to do the housecleaning and some sewing and, after that, make quilts.

Tonight, just before sundown, Diane and I, and Hannah in the baby carrier, strolled through Forget-Me-Not Lane to see the lovely sunset and to absorb the peace and beauty of the evening. The glory of the lowering sun was reflected in the water at the old swimming hole where the youngsters spent many hours this summer. Jared built a diving board and fastened a long rope on the willow tree leaning out over the water. Tonight

Diane said she wishes she could stay here forever, and I found myself wishing the same. We would miss them a lot if they had to leave.

> **Golden Gem for today:** *"I will lift up mine eyes unto the hills, from whence cometh my help. My help cometh from the Lord, which made heaven and earth." (Psalm 121:1-2). It is good to know that we can look to the Lord for all our needs, both spiritual and earthly.*

September 8

Billy had a bit of a setback and had to go back to the hospital. I guess he overdid things a bit. It's hard to keep a little boy that age from being too active. He seems to be taking it all in stride, though. Hannah and I went in with him again since the others are all so busy with the harvesting, and Sadie is busy home-schooling the other three children. We spent time in the playroom this afternoon and even got invited to a birthday party that was taking place there.

Konrad, a little boy who has been a patient in the hospital for several months (I don't know what his problem is), had a birthday today and the nurses had a surprise party for him. They came in carrying a big cake with eight lighted candles, singing "Happy Birthday To You" as Konrad was wheeled into the playroom in a wheelchair. On the table were paper cups of Hawaiian Punch and bowls of party mix to go with the cake. I believe Billy enjoyed the party as much as Konrad did, because he could talk of nothing else for awhile after we were back in his room. He tires easily and took a long nap, while I worked on embroidering a sampler patch Sadie gave me. Hannah slept peacefully, unaware of her surroundings, so I was glad to have something to do to keep my hands occupied.

September 9

The impatience on the north side of the house are a thing of beauty just now, with their pink and red blossoms covering almost the entire plant, and the row of flaming orange and yellow marigolds almost dazzles the eye. We have had more rain showers again recently, and they sure gave new life to the flowers, although they will soon succumb to Jack Frost.

Diane asked me to go along to the carriage shed tonight to show me how she had rearranged the playhouse she has there in the back room. She and Ginny spent quite a bit of time in there this summer happily fixing it up. They made a stove, refrigerator, and cupboards out of cardboard boxes, and even put little sliding drawers made from empty match boxes in the cupboard. The only furniture of real worth is the little table and two chairs that Sadie gave them.

The girls made cradles for their dolls by gluing rockers on round oatmeal containers. They even used thumbtacks to hang curtains at the playhouse windows which they made from old drapes Pam had given them.

While we were there, I heard a lot of thumping and bumping and scraping from upstairs and went to investigate. The four Grant children were there with Treva, who I thought was in her room hand-sewing her cape. They were all doing a major renovating job on the room that used to be an old office. Most of the things they used were brought over by the Grant children, with their dad's permission, they claimed. I hope that is true.

They laid an old brown and tan rug on the floor, cut to size with a utility knife; hung venetian blinds at the windows; put an old-fashioned round pedestal table in the middle of the room; and for storage, they had an old trunk from the Grants' attic. They had inverted apple crates for chairs and covered them with pieces of an old blanket for softer sitting (they said the extra one was for a guest).

The children were all quite enthused about their little project; they called it their clubhouse. They had formed a club called "The Good Deeds Club" and will meet there once a week to decide what good deeds for others they want to do the following week. They even made provisions for the coming cold weather—they brought up an old portable kerosene heater to use during their meetings. I asked them what kind of good deeds they planned to do, and for whom, and they said they will keep those things secret whenever they can, because there is more of a blessing when a good deed is done quietly. Well, they have the right idea and I hope they keep it up. Kermit thinks that with a bit of supervision, it should be all right.

> **Golden Gem for today:** *"The eternal God is thy refuge, and underneath are the everlasting arms"* *(Deuteronomy 33:27a)*

September 11

Today was blessedly cooler, one of those beautiful clear days where the distant mountains seem very near. Sadie spent the day at the hospital with Billy. He seems to feel okay, yet they want to watch him closely.

The Grant children weren't over at all yesterday, which is unusual. I can pretty well count on them dashing down the field lane soon after the school bus goes so they can help Kermit, Jared, Treva, and me with whatever we are doing. Groplie usually tags after them, looking for ways to either torment someone or to get into some kind of mischief. Pecking bare toes is one of his favorite things to do, along with pulling hair and squawking annoyingly. Perhaps the children will teach him to talk one of these days.

Today the Grant children came in the early afternoon, and they had two little girls with them. The two girls, ages six and seven, are friends of theirs and are staying overnight at their home. They were real little live wires, into everything, and we all heaved sighs of relief when they left. One of them chased all the chickens out of their pens, then ran noisily through the flock, shouting and clapping her hands while the chickens flew in all directions, squawking in alarm while the feathers flew. The other little girl dumped a lot of feed into the horses' stanchions, much to the boys' displeasure, because they had to quickly shovel it out again.

The girls then decided to help Treva mix cookie dough in the kitchen, and when Treva had her back turned, the youngest girl emptied a half-filled pitcher of milk into the bowl containing beaten eggs and melted butter. Treva lost her patience and ordered the child out of the kitchen. She ran into the sitting room where Diane and Ginny were sewing their quilt patches. The other little girl had a scrap of material and a needle and thread and wanted to learn to sew, but she soon tired of it and stuck her needle into the seat of the rocker cushion before running outside to find the boys. Along came the younger girl and flopped down on the rocker.

I was cutting grapes out by the grape arbor and heard the most horrible scream coming from the house. Rushing in to see what was wrong, I found the little girl rubbing her backside—she had sat on the needle! She quickly ran off, heading for the Grants' place. The older girl stayed to help get the grapes ready for juicing. I sent the girls down to the cellar to bring up empty jars, and I soon heard a series of yells, crashes, and breaking glass. The new girl had tripped on the stairs and fallen, dropping her jars, and bumped into Diane and Ginny, causing them to drop and break theirs, too (five in all!).

Whew! I'm glad those girls aren't our neighbors! The Grant girls suddenly seemed very well mannered and decent compared to them. Mr. Grant was over to see their clubhouse room a few days ago and gave his grudging approval.

"As long as it helps to keep you children out of mischief," he said. Mr. Grant seems so melancholy. Kermit talked to him for awhile, and the man seemed ready to share some of his troubles. His faith seems to be hiding behind a shell of bitterness. It's sad to think that at one time he was a minister and that he has no desire to continue in that profession. May God help him to find peace and acceptance of his lot in life.

> **Golden Gem for today:** *Aside from the necessary chastening, the trials of this life, painful and cruel as they may seem, are but a tender preparation for sanctification and fitting for the Master's service. Sometimes prayers are answered in a way that seems painful at first, but later the blessing is revealed, and God's wondrous plan is unveiled.*

September 15

Billy is home from the hospital! He came to our house instead of Uncle Nate's because Uncle Nate is having back trouble. Aunt Miriam has enough to do. What a welcome Billy received, showered with love and attention from his siblings and the Grants. They all want to do things for him; in fact, they almost fight over the privilege. Diane can hardly wait until it is time for Billy to open his next sunshine package tomorrow morning.

Treva made all his favorite foods for supper tonight, and Nola mixed a batch of his favorite cookies. They were disappointed that Billy didn't have much of an appetite. But he seems happy to be home, and it is such a blessing that he can be here.

Rudy and Barbianne came tonight, bringing a big wrapped package which contained games, puzzles, and books—things for Billy to do to prevent boredom. The children all had a jolly time at their favorite pastime, listening to Rudy's stories. He can make the characters come alive while the youngsters listen wide-eyed.

The Grant children came over later, each carrying a gift for Billy. It was just some of their outgrown toys, but they were treasures to him. Even Groplie seemed glad to have Billy home again, according to the attention he paid to Billy, pecking at his shoelaces and trying to untie them and making a general nuisance of himself. One of the books that Rudy and Barbianne gave was *Blackie the Crow*, and Ginny read it to the little ones. It appeared as if Groplie was listening intently, cocking his head to one side as if he understood the words. I liked the verses at the beginning of the chapters, such as:

> *When you're tempted to do wrong*
> *Is the time to prove you're strong.*
> *Shut your eyes and clench each fist;*
> *It will help you to resist.*

Another one was:

> *Judge no one by his style of dress;*
> *Your ignorance you thus confess.*

Also:

> *No greater happiness is won*
> *Than through a deed for others done.*

And:

> *When friends prove false, whom may we trust?*
> *The springs of faith are turned to dust.*

In the book *Blackie the Crow,* it sounded as if Blackie was wise enough to say those things and brought out some lessons for the children. We all enjoyed the story, not just the children.

It's time to get Billy to bed; it has been a tiring day for him.

September 16

Mom and Pop stopped in this afternoon because they heard about Billy's accident. They just came back from a trip to Lone Ridge. Instead of hiring a van, they had hitched two horses to the wagon and traveled at night to avoid traffic. It took awhile to get there, but they made it. They did have a scare, though, on the way home. It was as dark as pitch while they were traveling on a back road through a dense woods, and they were suddenly gripped with a feeling of foreboding, as if there were danger ahead.

They drove into a patch of fog so dense that they could hardly see the horses in front of them. Suddenly, the horses shied as a man jumped out of the woods and tried to grab the lead horse's bridle. With his other hand he whipped out a gun and demanded that they hand over their money. Pop lashed the horses with his whip and they reared up, then took off at top speed, leaving the man behind. The front hoof of one of the horses had knocked him down.

Mom and Dad stopped at the next little town and reported it to the police, and they stayed long enough to learn that the would-be robber was picked up by the police; he wasn't able to get away because his leg was injured. The robbery would have done the man little good—Mom and Pop had taken no money with them.

Hannah is quite *grittlich* these days, with her first little teeth pushing through. Tonight I put her in the stroller and wheeled her down Forget-Me-Not Lane to the creek. Silo filling has begun, and already a few of the earliest trees are beginning to change color. Squirrels chattered from treetops and crows called from their haunts in the woods. I wonder if Groplie will ever want to join his kind again.

It was all so lovely and peaceful, but Hannah still wasn't happy. So back up to the cherry tree swing we went, and Kermit joined us there. He took Hannah and soon had her laughing out loud. He tosses her up in the air, and she seems to love it.

Here's a poem I found in Barbianne's scrapbook:

> 'Tis so easy to love when your life is new,
> When for just a short while there's been two of you,
> When the china's unchipped and your small house shines,
> The windows are polished—the meals divine.
> Ah, then, 'tis so easy to love!
> But the love must stay, though the gloss is gone,

When the struggles come and the fight is on,
When nary a sunbeam gleams its way,
Through the low-hanging clouds from day to day,
But then, e'en then, you must love.

Thankfully, there are no low-hanging clouds on the horizon, except perhaps our financial difficulties. Soon I want to start making quilts to sell, and that should help to pay for groceries. Sometimes I wonder if we'll ever be able to buy property of our own. But I want to be content with our lot in life, for godliness with contentment is great gain.

Part Three

Good Deeds and Gratefulness

The Good Deeds Club members have been living up to their name. Jared, Jack, and Nick spent an evening doing odd jobs for Mr. Watson, our neighbor who has heart problems and needs to have surgery soon. He has a small farm, a few head of cattle, and some chickens and rabbits.

Mrs. Watson can't get around very well anymore, but she invited the boys in for lemonade and cookies. She told them she didn't know how she was going to get her fall housecleaning done and that it would probably take her until Christmas to do it.

Jared decided to give the girls a hint; it would be a chance for them to do a good deed, too. The girls were enthused about it, and this morning they headed for the Watsons' armed with buckets, mops, wash rags, pine oil, and a broom, planning to do Mrs. Watson's cleaning in a jiffy. But when they arrived, they were disappointed to find both the front and back doors locked. They were about to head back home when Nola got the bright idea of going in by way of the basement and doing the cleaning even though the Watsons weren't home. So they entered through the unlocked basement door, feeling like helpful brownies, ready to do a good deed secretly.

Mr. Watson's son had taken his dad to a doctor's appointment and Mrs. Watson had locked the doors and gone to her bedroom to rest. She fell asleep and was awakened by thumping noises in the basement and footsteps coming up the stairway. Burglars! was her first thought and she quickly dialed 911. She told the police to come at once because there were burglars in the house. She hurried up the stairs to the second floor as fast as her stiff joints allowed, and locked herself in the spare room. Thinking that the intruders might break in that room, too, she hid in the room's walk-in closet and locked that door.

The girls, unaware of the fright they had given Mrs. Watson, happily began to sweep and dust, feeling very virtuous. Molly was just heading for the door to shake out a rug, when she spied a police car heading in the driveway.

"Oh, no!" she gasped. "The police are coming! Maybe someone saw us sneaking into the house and called the police. Let's run upstairs and hide!"

The five girls needed no second invitation. Fear lent wings to their feet and they rushed up the stairs as fast as they could and ran down the hall into a back bedroom. They quickly closed and locked the door, and all of them scrambled under the bed and pulled the spread down a bit so they wouldn't be seen. There they hid, hearts thumping with fear, until the police finished searching the rest of the house and knocked on the door of the room they were in. They stayed as quiet as possible, thinking that the police would leave, but instead they forced open the door and soon discovered the trembling girls jammed under the bed. Mrs. Watson had come out of the closet by then, and when the officers told her that her burglars were just a bunch of frightened little girls, they all had a hearty (but shaky) laugh over it.

One by one the girls shamefacedly crawled out from under the bed and the police went away laughing, probably wishing that all their summons would be hilarious instead of dangerous. Mrs. Watson sincerely apologized for her error and had the girls sit at the table for a snack of milk and cookies before they resumed their housecleaning. She was very happy with all they got done by mid-afternoon when Mr. Watson returned.

Mrs. Watson took the girls upstairs to the very room they had hidden in and there, in a big china cabinet, showed them her collection of dolls. She unlocked the glass door and told them they could each choose a doll to take home. There were dolls of all sizes and descriptions—baby dolls, lady dolls with all kinds of accessories, dolls with long ringlets of curly hair, china dolls, dolls that could talk and cry, and Cabbage Patch dolls.

The girls thought they had never before seen such a marvelous sight and had a hard time choosing. They went home with shining eyes, delightfully happy with their gifts. Although they are a bit too old to play with dolls, they realize these dolls are apparently valuable collector's items. It made the boys grumble a bit that they had gotten nothing for the work they did, but this evening Mr. Watson stopped in and said he had another job for them. His eyes twinkled merrily when he added that he would have some "dolls" for them, too.

> **Golden Gem for today:** *Delay, until you are sure of God's guidance. Many Christians earnestly beseech God's help for the momentous decisions of life, but in the small things they forge ahead alone.*

Tonight as Nola was going down the cellar steps with a half-filled basket of eggs, she tripped and fell, smashing every egg. The egg yolks were all over her and her clothes were a soggy mess. When the other girls saw that she wasn't hurt, they burst out laughing. She glared at them indignantly and started for home to bathe and get clean clothes.

Kermit and I have decided that since the children are at our house so much of the time, we have the right to make some rules. One of them is that the girls must wear dresses of the proper length, and the boys may not wear shorts. They have complied with the rules, probably because they enjoy being here so much, and if they behave, we're glad for their help.

But as Nola ran out the door holding up her long, egg yoke-splattered dress, she called back, "It was this stupid long dress that made me fall!" She was soon back, wearing a clean dress of the same proper length, and in good spirits again.

After Billy had been in the hospital, Groplie became strictly his pet. They seem to understand each other, and I wouldn't be surprised if the crow were soon able to talk. His shiny black coat gleams with the luster of good health and grooming, and he is entirely housebroken (I think he trained himself).

It's time to quit my ramblings and get the kitchen straightened before bedtime. Tomorrow we'll have a busy day getting a lot of housecleaning done. The younger girls are a big help, but it goes so much faster when Treva rolls up her sleeves and pitches in with her scrub brush and elbow grease.

Let no uncharitable and unkind thoughts dwell in your heart. All towards whom you send loving and forgiving thoughts will be helped towards God by you.

I hope I never again have an uncharitable or unkind thought about anyone. I'm afraid I have had such, though, for Kermit has told me about things his mom did that weren't very nice, and ways in which she mistreated him. Some were rather hard to believe, and it has affected my feelings toward her. Kermit has forgiven her, though, and I want to do the same.

Three days ago we received a letter from Kermit's mom with a check included that is enough to pay our way to Montana to visit her. She even arranged transportation for us. A friend of hers, Mrs. Kerr, who lives in Philadelphia and wants to visit them in Montana, will take us along and bring us back again. We have our suitcases all packed and are looking forward to going. We'll see the Mullets, Ben and Rachel, Chuck at Tall Cedars Homestead, Mrs. Elegant and Beechwood Acres, and Emily.

Now we'll see what it's like to travel with an infant. There is so much to take: disposable diapers, clothes, blankets, etc. I'll take my journal because I want to remember every detail of the trip. These past few days have been rather hectic, but at last we're all ready and waiting.

I can't blame Kermit's mom for wanting to see her grand-daughter. She doesn't feel able to travel because of her health, and having us come to Montana is the only way she can get to see Hannah. I think it was kind and thoughtful of her to take an interest. I would feel very badly if she didn't want to see her granddaughter.

> **Bible verse for today:** *"He that dwelleth in the secret place of the Most High, shall abide under the shadow of the Almighty."*

October 2

We're on our way, speeding westward in Mrs. Kerr's minivan. Kermit and Hannah are sleeping, but I'm still wide awake and bright-eyed, not wanting to miss anything of the interesting scenery whizzing by. I'm thankful for every safe mile and am enjoying every minute of our trip. Hannah is doing so well; she must know we're going to see Grandma!

We stopped at a fast food place for lunch (hamburgers, french fries, and sodas), so I'm hoping we'll be able to have better fare for supper. I guess I'm just not used to that kind of food. A friendly couple from Australia came to talk to us while we were there. Mrs. Kerr is an interesting conversationalist, and she points out places of interest to us, which keeps things from getting boring.

I wonder how Treva and Jared are faring at home, keeping the shop going and the home fires burning. They plan to have their supper at Aunt Miriam's each evening, and Treva will stay there at night. I hope there won't be any burglars.

October 3

We stayed in a motel room last night, and my, we slept in such a wide bed. There was a crib for Hannah, but there would have been room for half a dozen children her size in our bed. Wow, such luxury! Deep carpets, elegant furnishings, electric lights which could be dimmed or brightened, a big television set which we, of course, did not turn on, and a big bathroom. That place seemed to have everything, including breakfast this morning. The scenery through the motel windows was pleasant, too, with mountains in the distance and a small lake in the valley, with a pair of swans swimming there. I would have liked to walk there because it looked so inviting. There was a low shrubbery hedge along the path, and a row of pines in the distance.

My thoughts travel homeward, and they also travel ahead to Montana. We'll soon be there!

> **Bible verse for today:** *"Commit thy way unto the Lord; trust also in him, and he shall bring it to pass"* (Psalm 37:5)

October 4, Sunday

Here we are at Tall Cedars Homestead! There's a spectacular sunset tonight with the last rays of the setting sun reflecting against the peaked mountains in the distance. The coyotes are eerily serenading us from the hills, yelping and howling, and the cattle are peacefully grazing on the foothills. If I was an artist, I would like to paint a picture of it, the whole majestic view.

We stood under the two towering cedar trees, listening to the wind sighing through the branches. Chuck took us on a tour of the farm, and it all brought back so many memories. We spent an enjoyable day with Kermit's mom, Stephanie, and Hunter; tonight they brought us here to spend the night in one of the bunkhouses.

Tomorrow we plan to visit the Mullets and Rachel and Ben. We'll tour Beechwood Acres and perhaps see Hal and Mirabelle. Kermit's mom was thrilled with her little granddaughter and took pictures as soon as we arrived. She's a doting grandmother, all right.

Golden Gem for today: *For a blessed day: Let your words be kind and gentle, your acts helpful, unselfish, and considerate, your hours filled with loving, unselfish ministering, and your heart the abode of sympathetic, kindly thoughts.*

October 9

The miles are swiftly flying by, and every moment brings us a little closer to Home, Sweet Home. We had a wonderful visit with the Mullet family, then Mrs. Elegant picked us up here and took us to see Beechwood Acres. We went to see Emily; her brother Ethan; and Mini, the ferret, who is still as bright-eyed and chipper as ever. They all thought that Hannah was the sweetest little thing they ever saw.

We spent the next night at the Mullets again, and the next morning we hitched their horse to the carriage and drove over to see Rachel and Ben. Their little boy Vernon is walking now and is really cute. It was so special seeing them and reliving old memories. After that, we spent more time with Kermit's mom.

Now we are almost home. Hannah did well, but she'll be glad to be home, too, and able to sleep in her own little bed.

October 11

Today is our fasting day—a day of reading the *Earnest Christian's Prayerbook* and meditating. It is also a day to read pages 105 to 107 in the *Lust Gartlein* and ponder the truths of the Word.

We arrived home yesterday to find that Sadie had planned a grand welcome home party! She and the rest of the family brought supper over, and the Rudys and the Grant children were also invited. Sadie made a great supper of oyster soup, homemade subs, freshly made cinnamon buns, and a freezer full of hand-cranked vanilla ice cream. Even Groplie the crow seemed glad to see us and flew on my shoulder as I walked to the house. But I suppose no one was more glad to see us than Treva and Jared.

The youngsters gave me an update on the Good Deeds Club, with the Grant children supplying much of the information. They had another adventure that turned out to be terrifying for them, but in the end everything was all right and they even made a new friend.

Our newest neighbors, the Detweilers, who moved to a farm two miles west of us, had announced a corn husking bee for Saturday afternoon the week Kermit, Hannah, and I left on our trip. It was not only for the youth of *rumshpringing* age, but also for anyone in the neighborhood who wanted to help. Kermit gave his permission for all our youngsters to go, and Mr. Grant said he thought it would be a good experience for his children to go, too.

They all trooped merrily across the meadow, because it was quite a shortcut if they went by way of the fields and woods instead of following the road. When they came up over a hill near their destination, they saw an old ramshackle homestead which was way back in the hills, with a lane over a half-mile long leading out to the road. The place was surrounded by a sagging, weather-beaten fence with some of the boards missing or broken; at some places the fence was patched with barbed wire.

The rambling house and the sheds surrounding it were as rickety and tumbledown as anything the children had ever seen. There was not a spot of paint on any of the buildings. Some of the windows were broken and others were missing entirely, with old sacks stuffed into the broken places and boards nailed over the missing ones. Battered and rusted implements and scrap iron were strewn throughout the barnyard and in the old fenced-in orchard in back of the barn. There was a flock of fine-looking sheep in the orchard—Jack said it was the only nice thing on the property.

The place had a kind of haunted and ghostly atmosphere and the youngsters skirted it as best they could, making a wide detour to the road. The dilapidated place couldn't be seen from the road, and if they hadn't taken the shortcut through the fields, they probably would never have discovered it.

They were tired on the way home after an afternoon of husking corn and decided to take the shortcut again to avoid too

much walking. They braved passing the rundown homestead again and discovered that the whole flock of sheep had broken out of their orchard pen and were in the field nearby.

The Good Deeds Club decided to live up to its name and chase those sheep back where they belonged. They saw that a portion of the fence had collapsed on its side and that was where the sheep got out. It would be a simple matter to set up that part of the fence and prop it up after the sheep were in. The youngsters set to work and rounded up the sheep and were herding them through the gap when they heard a man yelling angrily and saw a big dog come bounding toward them, barking ferociously. The man was shaking his fist and bellowing almost as loudly as the dog.

The children wasted no time—they took off running as fast as their trembling legs allowed and kept on running until they reached the next road, where they thought they were safe at last. But in a few minutes, a pickup truck came roaring toward them and the driver slammed on the brakes right in front of them. It was the same man who yelled at them, and their first thought was to take off running across the field.

The man stopped them by crying, "Don't run! I'm so sorry I yelled at you."

The children listened as the man continued. "At first I thought you were chasing my sheep and harassing them as some boys have done in the past. As soon as I realized that the fence was down and the direction you were herding the sheep, I knew better. I'm very sorry, and I want you all to hop on the back of my truck and I'll take you back to my place to finish the job. I'll treat you to cookies and lemonade, then take you all home, wherever you live. I want to make it up to you for treating you that way when you were only trying to help."

The man said he is a widower and his name is Eben. They couldn't remember his surname because it sounded a bit foreign. The girls were scared and went on home, but the four boys agreed to go with Eben. They helped to repair his fence, then, true to his word, he gave them refreshments. The inside of his house was surprisingly clean and cozy looking compared to the rest of the place. He was really friendly and told them a few entertaining stories, and even offered to pay them. The boys told Eben about their Good Deeds Club, and he enlisted their aid in chopping firewood for his stove this fall. He told them he would do a good deed for them in return—he had a surprise for them when the job was done. He didn't tell them what it was, but he did tell them they wouldn't be disappointed.

Bible verse for today: "Whosoever drinketh of the water that I shall give him shall never thirst; but the water that I shall give him shall be in him a well of water springing up into everlasting life." (John 4:14)

November 2

The beautiful, colorful autumn leaves have mostly fallen from the trees. After the rain and windstorm we had last week, the landscape appears stark and bare, all but the stately pines in the grove. The neighbor's pond is frozen over, but not solid enough for skating. The deer come browsing through the orchards looking for windfalls. Soon the hunting season will open; if they are wise, the deer will stay in the thickets.

Butchering is on the agenda this week; we're all out of meat and it's cold enough to butcher now. In spite of all the work and grease involved, it's a special time of working together with neighbors and making memories with the jovial bantering and visiting that goes on.

The Grant youngsters sure took a lively interest in the preparations to butcher the big hog we had fattened. They watched while Kermit sharpened the knives and scrubbed the big iron furnace kettle and washed and scalded the sausage grinder before fastening it to the saw horse.

The youngsters all declared they wanted a turn cranking the handle. Chuckling, Kermit told them they would soon have their fill of it. The Grants begged us to wait until Saturday to tackle the job so they would be off school and could watch. But it takes more than one day to finish and clean up, and since the next day would then be Sunday, we had to disappoint them.

But on butchering day, Mr. Grant arrived with the four children, giving them permission to stay home from school for something he terms educational. He stayed to watch and help a bit, becoming genial and friendly as the day passed. It seems as if we've only just gotten to know him, and he is really a very nice person under his gruff exterior. Hopefully, bit by bit, the shell of bitterness will peel off, his emotions will be healed, and he will go back to his calling of ministering to others. He certainly had a keen interest in the entire butchering procedure.

Kermit started a fire in the big furnace in the wash house to heat water for scalding the carcass. Mr. Grant lent a hand in hanging up the carcass and watched as Uncle Nate trimmed the hams and shoulders and squared the middlings. He and the children helped to grind some of the meat; Rudy sliced and salted some and stripped the fat for the lard. They set up a temporary smokehouse for curing the meat, then they will hang the meat from the crossbeams in the attic because of the lack of a smokehouse. We promised Mr. Grant some samples of sausage, bacon, and home-cured ham, and he was quite pleased.

Uncle Nate and Mr. Grant had some serious conversations, too, and the former minister shared some of his disillusionment and loss of faith. How could a just God take away the children's mother when she was needed so badly by her family? Uncle Nate had no answer for that, but he did tell Mr. Grant that his own mother died when he was young. God's grace had been sufficient for him and his father, and all things work together for good to them that love God. If his father would have become bitter and ceased to trust God and stopped serving Him, God wouldn't have been able to help Him.

This must have set Mr. Grant thinking deeply, because he was quiet for awhile. Soon, he gathered up his brood of children and went home. We must keep on praying for him.

The next thing to do is make doughnuts with the freshly rendered lard. Treva and the younger girls will help, and perhaps even Sadie will get a whiff of the scent of mounds of delectable golden brown, yeasty-smelling *fet-kucha* and come and join the party.

November 7

I had a letter from Grandma Annie today. She seemed a bit lonely, even though they are still able to go visiting. With our lively house full, I can't imagine what it will be like after all our fledglings have flown from the nest. I must try to write to Grandma more often. She keeps herself busy quilting, and they visit shut-ins frequently. In the November wedding season they are invited to weddings nearly every Tuesday and Thursday. She always adds helpful nuggets of wisdom and truth in her letters to bolster our spiritual life, and I just wish I could take them to heart better.

I'll copy here what she had at the end of her long letter. It's from a book by R. A. Torrey, *How to Obtain Fullness of Power.*

> *We cannot obtain power, and we cannot maintain power in our lives, and in our work for others, unless there is a deep and frequent meditation upon the Word of God. If our 'leaves' are not to wither, and whatsoever we do is to prosper, our delight must be in the law of the Lord and we must meditate therein day and night.*

I remember Grandma's worn Bible with many phrases underlined. She is a good example; she reads the Word daily and has a chart with guidelines for daily Bible reading that covers the whole Bible in one year. I will write to her tonight and ask her to pray for us, and we will do the same for her and Grandpa Dave.

November 13

We had mild Indian summer weather this week, and Eben had the boys make good use of it. They painted the outside of three of his sheds that are still in fairly good shape. Even Kermit spent an evening there repairing the porch and helping to paint. The boys also helped load pieces of scrap iron onto the back of Eben's pickup truck to take to the recycling center.

Eben asked Kermit to spray paint his house (with a borrowed sprayer) and Kermit kindly said he would. Now the house looks much better. We wondered at this sudden urge to fix up the farm after all these years. This evening another neighbor told us Eben is planning to take a wife, so that explains everything. He is not a poor man and must be quite generous, because the "good deed" he told the boys he would do for them in return for their help was certainly a valuable gift—a two-year-old colt! He kept a few horses as a hobby, and the colt was the last of them. Eben wanted it to have a good home.

The boys are delighted and have plans to train the colt for riding and driving. Eben was right: they certainly were not disappointed with his gift. The Good Deeds Club has had some ups and downs, but it has paid off in more ways than one. The boys had the satisfaction of having helped someone, and even though they had not expected to get paid, they were amply rewarded.

Mr. Grant came over tonight to see the colt and had a long talk with Kermit. He is ready to return to his church and has released his self-will and bitterness and wants to make amends. That means Mr. Grant will probably be moving his family back to where they came from. We will certainly miss them, especially the children, but his going back to the ministry is surely a cause for rejoicing.

The other day I discovered that Billy and Diane had the crow in the doll carriage, wrapped in a doll quilt and wearing a ruffled cap.

The children love Sadie, but since I am back home, they ask quite often if they can come over. Of course, they are always glad to be back at Sadie's, too. It reminds me of something I read in the book *Eight Cousins*, by Louisa Mae Alcott. I'll write what I remember of it:

> *Motherly hearts beat warm and wise in the breasts of maiden aunts, and these worthy creatures are a beautiful provision of nature for the cherishing of their nieces, nephews, and other children.*

They certainly get great comfort out of it and receive much innocent affection that would otherwise be lost. Of course, Sadie isn't an older maiden, she is a young one, and will probably be snatched up by some young man before long.

The boys are really pleased with their new colt and have decided to name him Rusty. They built a three-sided lean-to on the south side of the barn. The colt's feed and water trough are there and he has free access to the pasture. Rusty is a handsome, spirited creature and loves to gallop and trot around the pasture with his head high and his tail flying in the breeze, snorting and shaking his handsome head when anyone approaches him. He is quite up-headed and fleet-footed, but entirely too wild to suit the boys. They are trying to tame him by whistling to him from the rail fence. When he warily approaches, they try to entice him closer by offering an apple or a carrot. Several times a day I hear someone clumping down the outside cellar steps to where the carrots and apples are stored. If the boys continue, Rusty should be tame enough for training by spring.

Kermit has been working in his workshop full tilt after investing in some better tools. Funds are at an all-time low, and he must do something to keep bread on the table, as the expression goes. Paying for food isn't as much of a problem as the other bills. The cellar is well stocked for the winter, but those hospital bills set us back quite a bit. We both seem to need new boots, shoes, and clothes, and my bill at the fabric store was high because there is a lot of sewing that needs to be done for Hannah before spring.

We'll have to scrimp and save and make do, wear things out, and learn to do without. Use salt and baking soda instead of toothpaste; vinegar water instead of Windex; eat cooked cereals instead of expensive boxed ones; use homemade laundry soap, etc. Oh, well, there are worse things than being poor.

I think of the verse: "Seek ye first the kingdom of God, and all these things shall be added unto you." Maybe someday the hard times will ease, then we'll be able to return the favors others have been doing for us. The other morning we found a box of groceries on the back porch and we have no idea where it came from. Another time we received an envelope in the mail containing a twenty-dollar bill, and no one had signed their name. Some people other than the Good Deeds Club must quietly be doing good deeds. They shall have their reward, although doing good for others is its own reward.

> **Golden Gem for today:** *All who are in Christ are justified by the Blood of Christ. "Justified" means not only forgiven and cleansed, but reckoned positively righteous—the perfect righteousness of Christ is put to their account. In forgiveness they are stripped of the vile and stinking rags of their sins; in justification clothed upon with the glory and beauty of Christ, at liberty to serve God in freedom and joy, an accepted and beloved child of His.*

December 17

A month has passed since my last journal entry. Our wedding anniversary is past and Christmas is fast approaching.

Mom has sent over R. A. Torrey's book, and what I gleaned from it tonight encouraged and cheered me. I'll copy it here:

> *The Holy Spirit has power to renew men, or make men new. Regeneration is the Holy Spirit's work. He can take a man dead in trespasses and sins and make him alive. He can take a man whose mind is blind to the truth of God, whose will is at enmity with God and set on sin, whose affections are corrupt and vile, and transform that man, impart to him God's nature, so that he thinks God's thoughts, wills what God wills, loves what God loves, and hates what God hates.*

I am so thankful that Kermit, even though he came from a family that aren't church-going people, became a believer while he was at the Mullet home. He was willing to give his life to serving the Lord and being the humble, God-fearing, spiritual leader in our home. His goal is to raise our children in the nurture and admonition of the Lord.

Yes, we'll be able to say "children." If nothing unforeseen happens, there will be another little one in our family when Hannah is fourteen months old. We are very happy about it.

> *What is a baby? A baby is that which makes the home happier, love stronger, patience greater, hands busier, nights longer, days shorter, purses lighter, clothes shabbier, the past forgotten, and the future brighter.*

December 18

Aunt Miriam sent over a book entitled, *Touching Incidents and Remarkable Answers to Prayer.* It is heartwarming to read about how prayers were miraculously answered and faith rewarded.

One incident was about the experiences of a minister's family on the frontier. Every family there was struggling for survival, for times were hard. The minister needed an overcoat, and all their provisions were scanty. Christmas was coming and there were no presents for the children. His little girl prayed to get a doll, and the boys wanted skates. It seemed to the wife as if God had deserted them, but she kept her thoughts to herself because her husband worked so earnestly and heartily.

The morning before Christmas the minister was called to someone's home, and the wife packed a piece of bread for his lunch; it was the best she could do. She tried to whisper a promise of hope, but the words died on her lips.

The day seemed dark and hopeless, and when the minister returned, exhausted and chilled from the lack of adequate clothing, the last bit of her trust faded away.

The wife said, "I wouldn't treat a dog that way, let alone a faithful servant." Then, glancing up, she saw the lines and the look of despair on her husband's face, and felt that the promises of God were not true.

The couple sat in utter discouragement for an hour, then heard the sound of sleigh bells outside. Someone had sent a big box. There was a turkey; a bag of potatoes; a thick red blanket;

lots of clothing, including an overcoat the right size for the minister; skates for the boys; and a doll for the little girl.

It was as if at that moment Christ reproached them for not trusting Him. They knelt and asked for forgiveness, and sweet promises of tenderness and gladness flooded their souls. They were full of praise and gratitude, and wept for joy.

> ***Golden Gem for today:*** *Pray above all for the church of Christ, that it may be lifted out of its indifference, and that every believer may be brought to understand that the one object of his life is to help make the Saviour King on the earth.*

December 25

Hannah's first Christmas! She is taking her first steps, with Kermit holding her hands. We had Christmas dinner at my parents' home and had a very enjoyable day. Forget-Me-Not Lane, the meadowlands, and pine groves are all covered with lovely drifted snow. Lots of colorful birds are coming to the feeder these days.

Here is a poem for a child.

The Soul of a Child

The soul of a child is the loveliest flower
That grows in the garden of God.
It climbs from weakness to knowledge to power,
To the sky from the clay and the sod.
Toward beauty and kindness it grows on and on,
Neglected, it's ragged and wild;
It's a plant that is tender and wondrously rare,
The innocent soul of a child.
Be tender, O Gardener, and give it its share
Of love, of warmth, and of light,
And let it not lack for your painstaking care
A glad day will come when its blooms will unfold
It will seem that an angel has smiled,
Reflecting its sweetness and beauty untold
In the sensitive soul of a child.

Tonight Kermit brought in from the workshop his gift to Hannah—a small table and four chairs—just the right size for a toddler to have a tea party. My gift was a lovely, varnished glider rocker. All it needs is the cushion, and I can make that. Kermit is still the same kind and thoughtful husband.

When he came in from the barn, Kermit heard the sweet strains of Christmas carols being sung. It came from across the creek, wafting up the lane on the evening breeze. He hurried inside to tell me and I quickly stepped out on the porch and heard:

> *It came upon a midnight clear,*
> *That glorious song of old.*
> *With angels bending near the earth*
> *To touch their harps of gold.*

Peace on earth, good will toward men—what a beautiful, hopeful time of year, when the Christmas spirit of love abounds.

December 26

The whole Grant family came over tonight, including Mr. Grant and Bessie. They plan to move sometime within the next year, perhaps not until late summer, so we'll have them for neighbors for awhile yet. Mr. Grant is a changed man, it seems, and eager to get back to helping others. In the meantime, the Good Deeds Club can continue.

I'll write a little about Groplie—he's quite a crow, full of ginger and mischief! The children are teaching him to talk, and one thing he can say very clearly is *"Cum essa!"* It is not unusual to hear those words ringing out from the treetops at any time of day. He hasn't tricked anyone yet into coming in for dinner before it's time, but he probably will some day.

Groplie is now well able to fend for himself, but the youngsters still like to bring him tidbits of food, bread, and crackers. In summer, they provide the crow with tadpoles, minnows from the creek, and juicy grasshoppers. Groplie has been Billy's special pet ever since he was in the hospital. Sometimes Billy dresses up Groplie in a doll jacket and cap and takes him for a ride in the doll buggy. When the weather is bad, the crow shares the barn rafters with the banties.

Under Uncle Nate's tutelage, Jack, Nick, and Jared have been working on training Rusty, the colt Eben gave them. Nate loaned them the two-wheeled training cart, and although the colt is still

very young, he can already be hitched. I suppose with all that TLC and affection, Rusty just had to make rapid progress.

Before it started snowing, the boys could be seen almost every evening driving down Forget-Me-Not Lane with Rusty hitched to the cart, headed for Uncle Nate's farm. The colt is quite up-headed and handsome, and seeing him trotting or splashing through the creek is a pretty sight. Uncle Nate thinks he will be a good road horse, and the boys want to ride him, too.

Golden Gem for today: *Every precious spiritual blessing in our own lives is given by our Heavenly Father in answer to true prayer. Prayer promotes our own spiritual growth and our likeness to Christ as almost nothing else can. The more we spend in real, true prayer, the more we shall grow in likeness to our master, and the fullness of the Spirit, with an ever increasing and enriching volume of abundant blessing and overflowing praise.*

It makes me realize how very far my life is from what it should be and gives me a desire to have it be all it could be, cleansed from all sin and selfish earthly ambition. How glad we can be that the mercies of the Lord are new every morning.

January 1, New Year's Day

If joy thou bringest, straight to God the Giver
Our gratitude shall rise, for 'tis His gift,
If sorrow, still amid waves of grief's deep river
Our trembling hearts we'll to our Father lift.

The new year is before us with its precious hopes and unknown experiences, be they joyous or sorrowful. The wind is howling around the corners of the house, and more snow is predicted. I read a bit more in the book *Touching Incidents and Remarkable Answers to Prayer*, this time about a widow and her two daughters who were stranded in a New England snowstorm with their supply of fuel and food exhausted.

The mother's trust was built on a strong foundation, and she placed her burden on the everlasting arms. There was wind and snow in abundance, and the girls became alarmed.

The good mother said, "Don't worry, the Lord will provide."

A mile away a man sat by his fireside, surrounded by every bounty and comfort needed to cheer his heart. He began to have a strong conviction that he should take provision to the poor widow. He ordered the oxen yoked, put a sack of flour and a load of wood on the sled, and headed for the widow's home. The man's daughter had tried to dissuade him, but he felt that the Lord was sending him.

The oxen floundered through deep snowdrifts as they carried the load of wood and flour. When the widow heard him at the door and saw what he had brought, she was filled with joy.

The man said, "The Lord told me, sister, that you wanted some wood and flour."

"He told you the truth," the woman said, "and I will praise Him forever."

From that hour, the family learned to trust Him who cares for the needy in their hour of distress, and who, from His boundless stores, supplies the needs of those who trust in Him.

> **Golden Gem for today:** *Cast all your burdens upon the Lord, and He will sustain thee. How foolish is the disciple who contends with struggling to bear his own burdens, when there is only one place for them.*

February 13

The Grant children came over with homemade valentines for Chet, Diane, and Billy, and even a small red heart for Hannah with "I Love You" printed on it.

Kermit says that Mr. Grant is a changed man since he is again dedicating his life to the ministry. Even the children seem happier. It is no wonder they had spent so much time at our house—their father was morose and had no time for them. It is a miracle that he is now a devoted parent.

Billy is still an outdoor boy and likes such things as mice and bugs and interesting rocks and plants. He can hardly wait until spring comes. Sadie says that all three of them are doing well in their studies and are quick learners.

This evening Billy came bouncing into the kitchen with Groplie on his shoulder (they are together almost constantly) and said that he wishes he could stay here the rest of his life. Well, so do I, but it is not up to us.

Just then Groplie flew over to the kitchen counter and began pecking at the raisin pie I had just set out to cool. With a squawk of disgust, he flew back on Billy's shoulder—the pie was hot! The crow is still as mischievous as ever. Almost every day I will hear shouting and scolding over another one of his pranks. But everyone is quite fond of him. They get a big kick out of Groplie being able to say words, and his vocabulary continues to increase. Some of the words he can say are *"Cum essa,"* "Hello," "Good-bye," "Mam," "Dat," all the children's names, and his own name. They all sound surprisingly clear.

This evening after a mild day of intermittent rain, the sun shone through the falling raindrops, creating a bright, beautiful rainbow. I caught myself wishing there really was a pot of gold at the end of it (as Billy once thought), enough for us to buy this farmette at the end of Forget-Me-Not Lane. I sat there daydreaming about it and even had a name picked out, Forget-Me-Not Farmstead. But as soon as I had thought it I was ashamed of myself, for I know that what I really need (as Kermit said) is bushels of serenity and contentment, as described in the Serenity Prayer.

Lord, grant me the serenity to accept the things I cannot change, the courage to change the things I can, and the wisdom to know the difference.

Treva wrote a letter to her family last night, and on the back of the envelope along with the seal, she had written: May your life be a "Song of Serenity." I don't know where she got that, but I thought it was rather appropriate. If we have godliness with contentment, then our lives can be songs of serenity. But there are so many stumbling blocks to that goal and so often we fall by the wayside.

I think I'll copy a **Golden Gem** before I get back to work:

"Seek ye first the kingdom of God and his righteousness; and all these things shall be added unto you." (Matthew 6:33) Seek in all things the advance of God's kingdom. Live only for God's glory. Whatsoever ye do, do it all to the honor and glory of God. Know no values but spiritual values, no profits but that of spiritual gain. In this lies true happiness.

March 2

The Good Deeds Club seems to be thriving, and the youngsters have done a surprising amount of good. Even Mr. Grant has taken a big interest in their activities and drives them to and from their missions of mercy. He even goes out of his way to drum up good deeds for them to do.

Some of the things they have done after school and on Saturdays include feeding Mr. Watson's livestock and menagerie; babysitting for a young mother whose husband was in an accident; shoveling snow for an elderly man who had health problems; doing the laundry and cleaning for Mrs. Watson; and cleaning out Eben's garage. Last fall the children helped Rudy and Barbianne with their produce when they weren't busy with ours and did numerous other little jobs. It is a good experience for them to help others without expecting payment, although they've found that it is not as easy to do things in secret as they had first thought.

Rusty, the colt, is shaping up well, as mannerly as they come. Jared would like to buy out the others' share of the colt so it would be his for *rumshpringing* later on, and the others still could ride him sometimes if they wished.

Time to go; Hannah is stirring after her nap.

> **Golden Gem for today:** *The work of righteousness shall be peace, and the effect of righteousness serenity and assurance forever. Confidence and assurance is the peace born of a deep certainty in God, in His promises, in His power to save and keep you. Rest and live in Him.*

March 29

Pam Styer stopped in a few days ago and asked if we wanted to go along to Johnstown to see where the big dam broke in 1889 and to see the flood museums. We decided to take a day off for a change and go with her.

We started off at six o'clock this morning. Sadie, Chet, Diane, and Billy went along, too, and Hannah stayed with Aunt Miriam.

When we arrived at Johnstown, it was easy to see and understand why there had been so much damage and devastation centered there during the flood. There are high mountains on either side which prevent the water from spreading out. We drove first to where Lake Conemaugh had been and saw the two ends which are all that remain of the big earthen dam that was washed away in the flood of May 31, 1889.

Where the lake had been, there is now only a valley with a river flowing through the center. Grass grows where there had once been water sixty feet deep. The lake had been two and one-half miles long and a mile wide at some places, and we were told that it had contained approximately twenty million tons of water.

Next, we drove to Johnstown to see the flood museum. We watched a film about the flood and its cause. It showed a gang of workmen at the dam, working in the heavy rainfall with lightning flashing and thunder crashing, trying to make another spillway for the rapidly rising water in the lake. But the workmen couldn't accomplish much, and soon the rising water was flowing over the top of the dam, a dangerous situation.

The film showed a horse and rider galloping to South Fork to warn people that the dam was in danger of breaking. It's sad to say, but people didn't believe him. At 3:00 p.m. on that fateful day the dam broke. Seconds later, the entire dam erupted and a giant wall of water headed toward Johnstown. At 4:07 p.m., the people of Johnstown heard a deep, steady rumble that grew louder and louder until it roared like thunder. A thirty-six-foot-high wall of water, mud, trees, logs, rubbish, and wreckage from collapsed houses hit the city.

The devastation was like a nightmare. Buildings were swept off their foundations and dashed to pieces. At Woodvale, the trolley shed containing eighty-nine horses and thirty tons of hay was washed away. The flood water contained miles of barbed wire from the wire works, and people became hopelessly tangled in it.

The big wall of water hit the side of the mountain above the Stony Creek River, close to where the Stony Creek and Little Conemaugh Rivers join. This saved the railroad bridge below it from collapsing, and debris began to pile against its massive stone arches. Houses, boxcars, trees, animals, and hundreds of people— dead and alive—were driven against it, forming a mountain of rubble forty feet high. At 6:00 p.m. a fire started in this wreckage, possibly oil from a railroad car seeped down through the wreckage to overturned coal stoves in the mangled houses. There was such a huge fire that it burned for two days.

We took a ride on the Inclined Plane which took us up the side of the five-hundred-foot mountain. There we could see over the city of Johnstown, the two rivers and where they joined, and the railroad bridge against which all that rubbish had piled and created such a big fire.

Next we went to another museum where we saw the second film. It was rather frightening to see the people in their houses as they heard the rumbling water, and jumped up in alarm. A great wave of water burst through a window or door and swept the house away.

The film showed a man in a buggy trying to drive away from the great wall of water bearing down on him, but the water overtook him. The devastation lasted for ten minutes, then all was over except for the fire. The flood left indescribable destruction and anguish in its wake. Over 2,200 people died and 27,000 were left homeless. Ninety-nine entire families were wiped out, and many of the bodies were never found or identified.

In the literature I bought at the museum, it says that the survivors eventually recovered from the shock and went to work rebuilding the city. They said, "By God's grace we shall make the city more thriving than ever." Two babies born in Johnstown on May 31, 1889, were given the surname "Flood," and one was named Moses.

One of the magazines I bought showed a picture of the city of Johnstown a few years after the flood, and already great progress had been made in rebuilding the city.

The awful calamity that befell Johnstown on that fateful day so many years ago was terrible, yet the attack on the Twin Towers at the World Trade Center and on the Pentagon was so much worse because of the evil intentions that were behind it.

Hannah was so glad to see us when we got home this evening, and we were just as glad to see her. I had to think of the woman in the Johnstown flood who lost her husband and all eight of her children.

She said, "Oh, if only one had been spared . . . just one. . . ."

April 10

Kermit is plowing the field and we're having lovely springtime weather. The big apricot tree by the meadow fence is in blossom, and there is a flock of seagulls following the plow. The robins are joyously singing their songs of cheer, and a pair of cardinals have made the pine grove their home. Their sounds of "good cheer, good cheer," echo up Forget-Me-Not Lane. The grass is growing thick and green, and it is time to get the push mower out of the woodshed.

The midwife told me I should go for a walk every day, so every morning and evening, while Kermit watches Hannah, finds me heading down the lane. Sometimes if Kermit has time, he joins me and brings Hannah along. It is so delightful with the beauties of springtime all around us, the heady fragrance of green things growing, and the birds' sweet chorusing.

Yesterday Hannah started walking alone without holding on to the furniture, so she toddles around on her sturdy little legs. She can say "Mama" and "Dada," and waves bye-bye. Her hair has been growing faster lately; soon I'll be able to make bobbies.

This morning I walked all the way back to the *Ketta Shtake* and met Aunt Miriam coming to see me. She brought us an apple pie and some *Friendship* magazines to read. Aunt Miriam had some great news: Sadie had a date on Sunday night with a young man from Missouri. He is here to help an uncle while the uncle recovers from an injury. Well, well, I hope he's worthy of her—Sadie is a jewel.

Oh, good! There's a spring wagon coming in the lane. It's Mom, Pop, and all the family! What a good time for them to come. I have the apple pie to share with them and a freezer full of homemade ice cream that Jared cranked. Treva just made a batch of soft pretzels, too.

> Not rich in wealth am I, not rich in gold.
> But rich in happiness, blessings untold.

May 12

Today is Hannah's first birthday. We had a little party for her. Sadie brought Chet, Diane, and Billy over, and we had ice cream and a decorated cake with one candle on it. Treva had made the cake and the custard for the ice cream, which Kermit cranked. We topped the ice cream with butterscotch pecan topping that Sadie brought. It was delicious!

The children played games, and afterward they each handed Hannah a small, wrapped gift. Her big blue eyes opened wide, then a big smile lit her face. She is our precious little sunbeam.

Here is a poem I like:

First Birthday

One year ago upon this day
Our God looked down to bless,
And sent a little bundle here
To bring us happiness.
He knew the joy a baby brings,
He wished our hearts to fill;
He wished an increase in our love
And so He worked His will.

His will in us! With this result:
Our tiny baby dear.
Father, Thou has been good to us!
How great Thy works appear!
A year of precious baby ways,
Of hugs and smiles and coos,
A year of blessings from our God—
No better could we choose.

May 20

What a beautiful time of year when the birds are joyously singing, the lilacs blooming, apple trees laden with sweet, fragrant blossoms, frogs trebling in the swamp, garden vegetables coming up, and the breezes balmy and warm. The meadow grass is green and lush and full of a myriad of dancing buttercups.

While I was taking my daily walk down the lane this morning, I decided to sit by the creek for awhile, absorbing the peace and serenity of the morning. I sat on the big rock on the bank, half hidden by a canopy of foliage. Someone was singing! It was Sadie, singing softly as she came down the lane from the orchard.

Ich weiss nicht wass
Soll es bedeuten,
Dass Ich so traurig bin.

A moment later she saw me and her face lit with a smile.

I said, "What? You don't mean to tell me that you're *traurig* (sorrowful) on such a lovely May morning?"

Sadie came across the creek using the stepping stones, then sat beside me on the rock. "I am, though," she said. "I have an ache in my heart."

She went on to share her feelings and indecision about the young man she is dating. She doesn't feel that they are right for each other and doesn't want to continue seeing him but hates to hurt his feelings. I guess she mostly needed a listening ear, because I didn't know enough about the circumstances and couldn't give her any advice.

Before she got up to go, Sadie had made up her mind. She is going to terminate the friendship because she doesn't feel that it is God's will to continue it. That's too bad, because she would make a wonderful wife. But God's ways are not our ways, and each one must follow His leading.

Part Four

Gelassenheit

H appiness is . . .

- Kermit bringing in a bouquet of blooming roses for me.
- Weeding the entire garden patch before the thundershower arrives.
- Receiving a letter from the Mullets announcing their intention to visit us this fall.
- A bowl full of luscious, red-ripe strawberries.
- Sitting on the swing under the cherry tree, with Hannah romping on the lawn.
- Hannah happily bringing me a marigold (what is sweeter than a baby with a flower?).
- Visiting the midwife and being told that all is well.
- A meal of the first fresh peas from the garden.

R ain, rain, and more rain. This is the third day of rain, and the creek is looking more and more like a raging river overflowing its banks. There was a lull in the rain this afternoon, and I decided that was my chance to go for a walk.

Down through the grassy meadow I went, toward the dull roar that was the creek. I stood on the bank watching the muddy brown water rushing past, and every now and then I saw a bobbing log or a bit of wreckage whirling past.

My thoughts traveled to Great-grandmother Feronica's journal, where her stepmother Magdalena and Magdalena's first husband were swept away by flood waters. Magdalena had held on to tree branches for dear life. She was rescued, but her husband was carried away by the current and drowned. Six weeks later, a healthy baby boy was born to Magdalena.

Then I thought of the tragedy of the Johnstown flood where so many were swept away and drowned. Flood waters are an awesome, mighty force, so very powerful and destructive. I hope the *Ketta Shtake* won't wash away.

> **Golden Gem for today:** *The cross of Christ is the measure by which we know how much Christ loves us. That cross is the measure, too, of the love which we owe to the Christians around us. It is only as the love of Christ on the cross possesses our hearts and daily animates our whole being, that we shall be able to love one another.*

June 23

Still more rain. The swinging bridge did wash away when a big log crashed into the middle of it. The two ends were still there, seemingly undamaged, and if someone would have started across in the dark not knowing the center was gone, he would soon have stepped into mid-air and fallen into the raging currents below. That reminds me of the short story I read in *Touching Incidents and Remarkable Answers to Prayer.* I'll copy it here.

Only a Tallow Dip

The following was related in an evangelistic meeting: A woman who had been bedridden for years lived near the railroad track, a long way from any other house. Nearby was a deep gully over which the railroad passed on a new, substantial iron bridge, as was supposed. There was a terrible wind one night. This poor woman, as was often the case, was alone. All at once she heard a fearful crash; she felt sure it was the bridge. She looked at the clock. In ten minutes the through passenger train would be along. What should she do? Her son was away from home.

Praying earnestly to God for help, she took the only light in the house, a tallow candle, and began to crawl (for she could not walk) toward the railroad track. How she ever got there she never knew. The track reached, she could hear the roar of the coming train. She prayed this prayer: "O God, help me to light this candle and keep it burning until the engineer sees it; and make him see it."

God heard her prayer. The candle was lighted, there was a lull; just then she waved the candle—would the engineer see it? She heard a grating sound; she knew the brakes were set. She lost consciousness then, but the train came to a standstill a few feet from the yawning chasm. Hundreds of lives were saved. This weak, sick woman did what she could; God used what she had. He will use what you have for the saving of men, if you will do your part.— *Union Gospel News*

O Christian! If that poor woman felt so deeply the need, and made so great an effort, to save the passengers of that train from physical death, how ought you to feel, and what effort ought you to make, in order to rescue the multitudes about you that are hurrying on to eternal ruin unconscious of their danger and ready to perish, unless someone, who has the light and knowledge, goes to their rescue?

> **Golden Gem for today:** *The power of union we see everywhere in nature. How feeble is a drop of rain as it falls to earth. But when many drops are united in one stream, and thus become one body, how speedily the power is irresistible. Such is the power in true union in prayer.*

June 24

Sunshine at last—fresh breezes are blowing from the west, and our mini-flood is over. The menfolks in the neighborhood got together first thing today to fix the *Ketta Shtake,* because the water there is always too deep to cross on steppingstones. The sounds of hammering and sawing came from that direction, along with the delightful, fragrant summer breeze and the joyous singing of the birds—probably they were as happy to have lovely weather as we. At ten o'clock Sadie came traipsing down the lane carrying two containers of cookies. She came to the porch where I was sitting on the old wooden rocker shelling peas, and said she needed help with the tea and lemonade for the men.

I got up and was about to say that I would help—I hadn't had my daily walk yet—when I remembered that parading down there in my condition wouldn't be proper, so I sent Treva to help. I suppose sometime I will be lithe and slender again.

Golden Gem for today: *All those who are under-*
taking a great thing have to prepare themselves, and
summon all their powers to their aid, and so Christians
need to prepare themselves to pray "with their whole
heart and strength." Prayer needs sacrifice of ease, of
time, of self. The secret of powerful prayer is sacrifice.

June 25

The four Grant children and Chet, Diane, and Billy are together more than ever these days because they know their time is short. The Grants are moving before too long, possibly in August, or even the last week in July. They help us with the strawberries, peas, weeding in the patch, and whatever we are doing, as fast as they can, then they run off down Forget-Me-Not Lane to play in the little dell near the creek where the ferns grow green and lacey.

Luckily, the flood waters didn't reach their *Shpiel Haus* (play house), as Treva calls it. It's on a bank above the creek. They made a table there by putting a formica-covered board that Kermit cut out of a sink counter top, on top of a stump. The children cleared a grassy area of stones and twigs and built a small stone fireplace at one side.

Nick dug a small hole near the big sycamore tree and put in a tin cookie container. He covered everything except the lid, then scattered dried leaves on top so it is invisible. It is their secret mailbox where they leave notes for each other on the days they can't come to play.

Diane said it reminds her of the island where they had a range shelter home at our Beechwood Acres farm, except there is no house there. There are winding fairy paths here and there, and when the wild cherry trees were in blossom it looked enchanting and delightful. The children know where all the birds' nests are and where the bunnies and woodchucks live. Squirrels scold them from gnarled branches of the big white-barked tree that reach out over the water. Chickadees gather in the wild rose bushes growing in the green undergrowth.

Pam Styer visited the place a few weeks ago (Sadie took her there), and she was so thrilled with it that she donated the white bench she had in her backyard. It looks like stone but

is made of some lightweight vinyl material.

Jack and Nick have plans to build a little hut or cabin there soon. They are so keenly interested in their project that they are sorry they soon have to move. Jared and Chet say they will finish the project if it is not done by the time the Grants have to leave. The girls have plans to make curtains for the windows and to get throw rugs, a tablecloth, and other homey touches for the cabin.

Early this morning Kermit left for Montana. Last night we received a telephone message via Pam Styer, telling us that Kermit's brother Kal had lost his life yesterday while deep-sea diving. No details were given, so I will have to wait until Kermit comes back to find out more. It was a shock, and even though they weren't very close it is still hard for Kermit to accept. I wish I could be with him.

We miss him so much. Hannah was walking around tonight asking, "*Dada, wu bisht?*" (Daddy, where are you?) in a sad little voice.

Baby was fussy today, but at last he is settled down to a peaceful sleep. I just tucked Hannah in, too, and now the household is quiet.

I'll copy a poem that is fitting with Kermit gone.

> *Linger not long, home is not home without thee:*
> *Its dearest tokens do but make me mourn.*
> *O, let its memory, like a chain about thee,*
> *Gently compel and hasten thy return!*

"Lo, I am with you always, even unto the end of the world." (Matthew 28:20)

Kermit is home, and he had a lot to tell me. His brother's death was a sad occasion for his family. He was glad to be able to spend some time with his second family, the Mullets. In about two months the Mullets will be heading east to visit relatives here and us, too! We're looking forward to their visit.

My parents and family came tonight, bringing the makings for a haystack supper and some fresh blueberries. They were eager to hear about Kermit's trip.

Baby was a bit fussy and his grandpa walked the floor with him. Grandpa seems proud to have a namesake and said he wants to give the baby a special gift. I wonder what it is.

While my family was here, another carriage drove in—Rudy

and Barbianne. How thankful we are for the kindness of friends and relatives in times of bereavement.

July 24

I had written to Rachel to let her know about the birth of our son and to send congratulations on the birth of their little Benjamin. She sent me a lengthy letter by return mail, bless her heart! She also sent *Beatitudes for a Wife*. I can just picture Rachel in her home, the epitome of virtue and blessedness, and I, too, want to follow these beatitudes daily.

1. *Blessed is she whose daily tasks are a labor of love; for her willing hands and happy heart translate duty into privilege, and her labor becomes a service to God and all mankind.*
2. *Blessed is she who opens the door to welcome both stranger and well-loved friend; for gracious hospitality is a test of brotherly love.*
3. *Blessed is she who mends stockings and toys and a broken heart; for her understanding is a balm to humanity.*
4. *Blessed is she who scours and scrubs; for well she knows that cleanliness is one expression of godliness.*
5. *Blessed is she whom children love; for the love of a child is more to be valued than fortune or fame.*
6. *Blessed is she who sings at her work; for music lightens the heaviest load and brightens the dullest chore.*
7. *Blessed is she who dusts away doubt and fear and sweeps out the cobwebs of confusion; for her faith will triumph over all adversity.*
8. *Blessed is she who serves laughter and smiles with every meal; for her buoyancy of spirit is an aid to mental and physical digestion.*
9. *Blessed is she who preserves the sanctity of a Christian home; for hers is a sacred trust that crowns her dignity.*

August 3

Billy and Diane haven't been over nearly as much since the Grant children moved away last week, but Chet comes over every evening. He and Jared hitch up Rusty, the colt, to the two-wheeled cart and go for a drive out the lane and back. They are not yet allowed to go on the road with him, so they are glad to have the lane. Rusty is doing well and seems to have the makings of an excellent road horse.

Baby is growing nicely. When the midwife stopped in last time, she said the baby seems to be in exuberant health. He's already two and one-half pounds heavier than Hannah was at that age, but he had a bigger start. Even his elbows and knees are getting dimples and his cheeks are chubby—the picture of a well-fed baby. Kermit has already been able to get him to smile.

Here's a poem for Baby.

> *A baby's a bundle of mirth and might*
> *With a nose as rosy as candlelight,*
> *Two eyes as bright as shining stars,*
> *And a hum like the strum of soft guitars.*
>
> *A baby's a blossom, a babble and coo,*
> *Your wealth and your world when day is through.*
> *I think God smiled when He cast the mold,*
> *For He packaged sunlight and warmth and gold*
>
> *Into a fondling, small as an elf,*
> *So folks could forget their troubles and self*
> *And live to hope and love and see*
> *A child . . . a fabulous fantasy.*

August 4

A new family has moved into the house the Grants vacated, an older couple with children who no longer live at home.

For the first time since my confinement I walked to Sycamore Hollow, the youngsters' grassy *Shpiel Haus*. I was amazed at the changes that had been made. With Sadie's help, the children had planted impatiens and coleus here and there among the ferns and made a stone path from Forget-Me-Not Lane to their hideaway glade. But the most amazing of all was the sturdy, sizable hut the boys had built in a clearing among the trees. It has a hinged door, cut-out windows, and a roof. The rock path looks almost like cobblestones and leads right up to the door. They had planted a honeysuckle vine on each side of the door post. A large, brass-colored urn stood to one side of the doorway, and in it was planted a clump of green ferns.

I had to stoop to get inside the cabin, but once inside it was surprisingly roomy. Another "stump" table with a Formica top stood in the center. Jack had made bookshelves for one wall, but there aren't any books on them. They have to wait until there is Plexiglas over the windows. A white tin cabinet that Rudy donated stands against the other wall. The floor has linoleum, paid for by Sadie. How typical of her to unselfishly donate time and money to help the youngsters with their project.

The children had a farewell party at their cabin for the Grant family the day before they left. They had an iced and decorated cake and a freezer full of peach ice cream, made by Sadie. We were invited, too, and it *shpeided* me that we couldn't go. Baby was feverish and fussy that day and we had the doctor come out to examine him. I was so glad the baby was better the next day, because it is such a helpless feeling when such a tiny one isn't well.

I haven't been using my baby's name. I just call him Baby, because I haven't gotten used to either of his names yet. I didn't want to hurt Kermit's feelings, so I agreed to his choice. I'm sure I shall soon learn to love both names and they will suit Baby to a "T." If you love someone, you love their name, too. Baby's grandpa was so pleased to have a namesake, and that's worth a lot, too.

August 22

The cornstalks are so tall this year that if I stand beside a cornfield I feel entirely dwarfed. The sky is very blue today, filled with puffy white clouds, and the tall trees along the creek are etched so clearly against the skyline. It almost reminds me of the big trees and big, blue sky in Montana.

Today I had a different sort of day—away from home. Grandma Annie's arthritis took a turn for the worse, and since she and Grandpa Dave have no children, the neighbor ladies are taking turns helping her for a few days. Today it was my turn and I could easily go since Baby is six weeks old now and I could take him along while Treva watched Hannah.

I enjoyed the day. Annie was feeling better again and Grandpa Dave was chipper, as usual, and in a storytelling mood.

He remembers his younger days better than recent events. They fussed over the baby and Annie even held him for awhile. They are such a dear old couple.

One of the stories Grandpa Dave told was of long ago when a group of Mennonites were being persecuted and driven from their homeland. The large group of refugees were heading for another country, fleeing for their lives. Families became separated and husbands and wives lost each other in the crowd. When the destination was reached, all efforts were made to locate their loved ones but they weren't always successful. If, after seven years of searching a marriage partner had not yet been found, it was a foregone conclusion that the spouse had died. The brethren had adopted a policy of allowing such persons to remarry.

One man searched for his wife for seven years and still had not found her, but he had a strong feeling that she was still living. He continued his search for many years, living the life of a wanderer, moving from place to place, and asking for her everywhere he went. And then one evening he found her. Someone had been able to give the man information about where his wife lived, but thought she had remarried. With a heavy heart the man made his way to the house, glad that there was no barking dog to give him away as he stealthily crept near in the darkness. He went to the back of the house where a light shone from the window, went as close as he dared without being seen, and looked in the window.

A family was eating supper. A man sat at the head of the table and a toddler about two years old sat on a stool next to him. Around the corner of the table with her back toward him sat a young woman holding a tiny baby, and there were several other children sitting in a row on the bench. The man reached over to a shelf and got down a big Bible and began to read aloud. After he had read a few verses, he replaced the Bible and they bowed their heads to say grace.

The heart of the man standing outside the window seemed torn in two because he saw there was something familiar about the curve of the woman's neck and the way her hair was swept up.

Was this his long lost wife, his bride? They had been married only six weeks when they became separated. He caught his breath as she got up from the table, turned around, and faced him to get something off a shelf. At first he felt great joy, then overwhelming anguish flowed through him when he saw that it was indeed his wife, and that she, thinking that he was dead, was married to another man.

With all his heart, he wanted to rush in and claim her, but something held him back. He moved away from the house, stumbling, as tears blinded his eyes. The children that he saw through the window needed both their father and their mother. If he revealed himself, the man in the house would feel more anguish than he did right now, and his wife's anguish might be just as great. If he left now, the woman need not know about his unhappiness. He quietly left and went far away, never to return. He built himself a little house in the mountains and lived like a hermit the rest of his days.

It is a sad story. It would have been just as bad to lose one's child, sadder than knowing the child is safe in heaven. But in heaven, all tears will be wiped away.

August 29

Chet and Diane are genuinely puzzled at the goings-on in their *Shpiel Haus*, Sycamore Hollow. Since the Grant family moved away, the old cookie tin secret mailbox had been unused. Then one morning Diane decided to look inside and found a note. There was a little poem written on it.

> *The sky is blue, the grass is green,*
> *I watch you play, your friend unseen,*
> *I share your little clubhouse fine—*
> *When you go home, then it is mine!*
> - Your Unseen Friend

The youngsters questioned just about everyone they knew in the area and all claimed they were not responsible for the poem. They were so curious about who might have left the note in the secret mailbox that Chet even talked of staying in the cabin all night, hiding under the table with its oversized tablecloth to see who was sharing their hideout. One morning they found a bouquet of zinnias on the table, and another time they found a bowl of M & M candy. The children are determined to somehow or other find out who is their mysterious visitor.

Baby is doing fine and is chubbier than ever. When I bathe him, I have to make sure I don't forget any creases. He smiles so sweetly and is so *brauuv* now. This poem is a reminder that this stage of babyhood won't last forever.

Yours For Awhile

Oh, little young mother, while gazing tonight
Down on that curly-haired one
Who sleeps so peacefully there in his crib
Remember that while he's your son
He's yours to keep only for awhile
For when he has grown quite tall,
He'll walk through the door and down the lane—
The world outside will call.

There comes a time he must go his way,
You've taught him the best that you knew
And out of the still of many a night
You've prayed he would always be true—
True to the things you thought the best,
True to his God and to you;
But, little young mother, the time will come
When he must choose what to do.

The time of decision may be dark for you—
For he may not see things your way
And lest you fill that moment with tears
Remember, oh, remember today
Little young mother, while gazing just now
Down on that curly-haired one,
He's yours for only such a short time—
Yours for an hour—your son.

August 31

No earthly queen upon her throne,
Hath greater power to bless,
Than she who daily makes her home
A place of happiness.

That poem comes from Rachel; I received a letter from her today. She is very busy with her two little boys and helping on the farm, and she doesn't have someone like Treva to help. Treva spends the greater part of the day in the woodworking shop now since I am able to work again.

Kermit is so busy in the shop now that he needs his two helpers. I can sense that it is really not what he likes to do, though. He doesn't complain, but sometimes it rather worries me. Tonight he joined me on the swing under the cherry tree and he seemed tired.

He muttered something about "Sawing, sanding, nailing, gluing, varnishing—that's all I do—and it's not really living. How much of the great and glorious outdoors I miss every day."

I murmured some soothing platitude and he soon was feeling more lighthearted, but my own burden was heavier.

"Casting all your cares upon Him, for He careth for you," is a comforting reminder.

September 1

They say that mothers have no pay,
But sonny smiled at me today,
And daughter stopped and hugged me tight,
As I went in to say goodnight.

It's silo-filling time again, and tonight as I sat on the swing with Baby on one arm and Hannah on the other, we heard the drone of the harvester in the neighboring field. We will soon have more wide-open spaces here in our hideaway behind trees and cornfields.

The row of orange marigolds along the carriage shed is flaunting vivid colors, and the pumpkins are ripening. Today I saw an early flock of wild geese winging their way overhead, and next month we'll have fresh cider. It was so warm there on the swing that we stayed until the large orange full moon came up over the treetops.

Kermit and his helpers were finishing a rush order, so we sat until it was done. Crickets were chirping and far away a dog was howling, reminding me of the eerie yelping and howling of the coyotes in Montana.

I happened to glance down Forget-Me-Not Lane and at that moment I thought I saw a movement in the shadows—was it someone coming our way? It was kind of late for Sadie to be coming.

I leaned forward, trying to see better, and just then a shaft of moonlight lightened the darkness—it was a shadowy figure heading toward the pine grove. I waited awhile, wondering who would appear out of the trees on the other side, but no one ever did. I watched and waited in vain, but whomever it was must have changed his mind.

Hannah's bright chattering and prattle eventually distracted me, and then Kermit joined us. He caught Hannah up in a bear hug, then tossed her up in the air and caught her. If there had been a thief, Hannah's shouts of laughter would have frightened him away. I mentioned to Kermit what I had seen, but he dismissed it lightly saying that maybe Chet was out.

In the evening when Kermit is done with the work is the best time of our day, when the rush and work and worry of the day is past. He is telling Hannah her bedtime story now and holding Baby at the same time.

September 3

Chet, Billy, and Diane came frisking up Forget-Me-Not Lane tonight, with more stories about mysterious goings-on in Sycamore Hollow. They found another note with a poem on it in the secret mailbox. Diane read it to me.

> *The leaves are falling—the ferns are brown,*
> *The birds are flying all around.*
> *While on the bench, your secret friend*
> *To you good wishes kindly sends.*
> - Your Unseen Friend

He or she must have been referring to the bench Pam donated to the *Shpiel Haus*. Perhaps the person sat on the bench while composing the poem. It sure makes me wonder who his or her secret friend might be. He or she had left a bouquet of marigolds and a small basket containing three packages of Twinkies.

Golden Gem for today: *The characteristic of love is that she seeketh not her own. She finds her happiness in giving to others; she sacrifices herself wholly for others. Even so Christ offered Himself upon the cross to bring that love to us and to win our hearts.*

Sadie had been preparing her lessons for another year of home schooling the three youngsters in their care, but their aunt arrived this afternoon and told the children to get ready to leave in two weeks. She will be taking them with her to her home in Georgia when she returns from a business trip. They will attend a private school there. Two weeks! At first it was a shock to the children, but now they are eagerly looking forward to the new adventure in their lives and have already started to pack their tote bags. After they are gone, the grass and weeds may grow a bit taller on Forget-Me-Not Lane because their running footsteps will be gone.

Hannah is lisping new words every day and even putting two words together. She can say her own name, but it sounds more like Anna. So we have started to call her Anna sometimes. Baby now spends a good bit of time in his musical, wind-up swing and sometimes even falls asleep in it. He is so sweet and cuddly.

> *Motherhood is the light in the eyes of a little girl as she plays with her favorite doll. Later, when the doll is carefully packed away with other childhood dreams, motherhood becomes the warmth of a tiny head pressed against a woman's heart and a moist little hand tightly clenching her finger. It is a feeling of wonderment . . . the awesome realization that this tiny bundle of perpetual motion is a life that she has created and delivered into the world . . . a human soul entrusted to her care. At times it may seem to be the most nerve-wracking, frustrating, heartbreaking, confusing joy in the world and she may find herself asking if motherhood isn't merely a polite word for pandemonium . . . until those golden moments when this child she has fed, buttoned and bathed . . . and scolded . . . climbs into her lap, looks into her eyes, and says softly . . . "I love you, Mother." Then she knows that motherhood is the most wonderful, rewarding thing that can happen to any woman . . . and she finds her heart whispering . . . "Thank You, God."*

This morning while the children were still sleeping, I went for a walk down to the creek to see the youngsters' Sycamore

Hollow. Blue jays were calling from the treetops, and a pair of squirrels frisked up a pine tree. The world was washed sparkling clean from yesterday's rain, and the air was crisp and fresh with gossamer spider webs spun from leaf to leaf on the wildflowers by the wayside.

I crossed the creek on the stepping stones and noticed that leaves were gently falling, floating downward on the breeze and sailing away on the water. I followed a winding fairy path through misty, sun-dappled woods and went the long way around to the hollow. It seemed almost like an enchanted cathedral, and I slipped into it and sat on Pam's bench, breathing in the woodsy fragrance and admiring the glistening, jeweled dewdrops. What a lovely, peaceful place to commune with God and ask for cleansing from the sins and stains of everyday living.

I was lost in thought when I heard a stirring in the cabin. The door opened, and out stepped a boy I had never seen before. He was tall and slender and could not have been more than twelve or thirteen years old. He had a mop of dark curls, nice delicate features, and big, dark eyes. He turned his head and saw me and a look of startled fear crossed his face.

"Hello!" I said in my friendliest voice. "Are you the secret friend who has been putting notes into the underground mailbox?"

The guilty look on his face was replaced by relief at my smile and friendliness, and he nodded his head. "I'm sorry I was trespassing," he said politely. "My name is Jeffrey Elgin and I'm staying with my grandparents who live just across the field from here. They just moved in a month ago." (So they were the new people in the house the Grants vacated.)

"I'm leaving for home tomorrow," the boy shyly said. "Could you tell those kids who often come down to this place that I want to thank them for the times I used the clubhouse and the bench. I always hid in the bushes whenever I saw them coming."

"I sure will," I told him. "You should have joined them— they would have been glad for company."

Jeffrey nodded. "I wish now that I would have. But I'm going to spend next summer with my grandparents again and then I'll be sure to make their acquaintance." I smiled and nodded but did not reply because I had no way of knowing if Chet, Diane, and Billy would be back for such a long stay next summer or ever again.

We bade each other goodbye, and as I headed back to the
stepping stones I heard voices from Uncle Nate's orchard. Sadie
and the three youngsters were making their way down the lane.
Their faces lit up when I told them I had discovered their secret
friend in the cabin and made his acquaintance. They were dismayed
that he would be leaving without their having talked with him, so we
planned a supper in the hollow—a farewell party for them and for
Jeffrey. Sadie volunteered to make lasagna and to bring a cake, and
I said I would make sandwiches and bring fruit and cold mint tea.

All three of the youngsters headed straight for the Elgin place to invite Jeffrey to the supper and were soon back, happy with the promise that he would come.

Sadie decided that we might as well make a real party out of it, so we invited my parents and family, Aunt Miriam and Uncle Nate and the boys, and Rudy, Barbianne, and Pam. They each brought something to eat, too, so we had a real picnic. It was a lovely warm evening, warm enough for babies, so Henry Luke had his first picnic. Jeffrey came as he had promised, bringing a Tupperware container of pecan tarts. We had to enlarge the hollow a bit to make room for all the lawn chairs.

Jeffrey and Chet were soon chatting away like old friends and wished they had gotten acquainted sooner.

Billy went wading in the creek and Sadie joined him, taking Hannah along. It was an evening of fun and fellowship, wonderful memories for our "memory chest." When it began to get dark, we sang a few songs: "In the Sweet By and By," "Where the Roses Never Fade," "I'll be Somewhere Listening," and "Twilight is Stealing."

Jeffrey admitted that he was the one who had been trespassing in the lane that evening I had been on the swing and had seen someone. He had thought no one would see him. I am glad he wasn't a burglar!

September 18

It seems really quiet around here with the youngsters gone. Soon it will be even quieter because the Mullets will be arriving for a visit in ten days, and when they leave, Treva and Jared will travel home with them for a month's vacation. We are in the midst of housecleaning in order to have everything spick n' span when the Mullets arrive. While cleaning out a drawer, I came across a poem I liked which I will copy here.

Take Time For Love

Take time for love; the days go by so swiftly,
And flown are those first days and weeks and years.
They're gone—too late to smile for last week's greetings,
Too late to sympathize with last month's tears!

Today! Take your beloved to your heart now!
Enjoy each other through youth's struggling days.
Don't be too grim to just have fun together,
And so face life with courage and with praise.

Take time for love; the baby now so cuddly,
So helpless! Constant are its small demands.
And yet, take time! Take time to still enjoy him,
Nor let tired crossness rush your loving hands.

His babyhood is short. Soon he'll be changing,
More independent: Time again to choose
For polishing and doing all the small things
That will intrude now, if you don't refuse.

Take time for love: the tiny one is growing
Into a toddler with an appetite
For life and learning and the curious art
Of mischief! Stop and play with him a mite.

Once in awhile take snapshot memories;
Keep baby books to write the big days on—
The First prayer, and the song he learned to sing with—
For barren days to come when he is gone.

Take time for daughter, too, and each in turn.
When school days come, still pal with them and smile.
Take time for love till they are on their own.
The loving times are such a little while!
                              - Almeta Hilty Good

I know that precious childhood years are fleeting, so I will cherish every moment with my children and jot down the golden moments for the time when memories will fade.

September 25

Bible verse for today: "Love not the world, neither the things that are in the world. If any man love the world, the love of the Father is not in him." (1 John 2:15)

The Mullets were here and stayed two days. Now that they are gone and have taken Treva and Jared with them, the place seems quiet and a bit lonely. We had a wonderful visit with

Kermit's "foster parents," and seeing them again brought back a lot of memories.

Pop Mullet said that he bought a big cattle farm similar to Tall Cedars Homestead (it is ten miles away from their home). He bought it because he felt it was a bargain and now he needs someone to farm it until his oldest boy gets married, which won't be for at least five or six years. He wondered if Kermit and I would be interested in moving back to their new cattle farm in Montana since Kermit has farming experience. Kermit's face lit at the suggestion, but when he looked at me and saw me shake my head and frown, the light in his eyes dimmed. I have no desire to move back to Montana after living here for only two years. I like being close to my family and to Aunt Miriam, Uncle Nate, and Sadie.

After the Mullets retired for the night, Kermit pleadingly said to me, "Just think. Moving to Montana would be a chance to be in the great outdoors most of the day under the big, blue sky and wide open spaces, horseback riding and rounding up cattle." You could see the eagerness in his eyes and could tell it was in his heart.

I turned away and said a trifle saucily, "Did you like being tossed to the ground by that big bull? Don't you remember how it felt to be out in the pasture in ten-degree-below-zero weather, floundering in the snow?"

But Kermit seemed not to hear and went on in a dreamy voice, "Don't you sometimes long to hear the coyotes howling in the evening, the whippoorwills calling from the plains, or the wind sighing through the cedars? We could really live there and I'd be out in the open spaces rather than in the stuffy woodworking shop."

When I continued to obstinately shake my head, the brightness in his eyes faded. He turned away and went outside to close the barn door.

I feel bad now about the way I acted, but Kermit will probably soon get over it. I hope neither he nor Pop Mullet brings up the subject again. It was fine living at Tall Cedars Homestead when we were on our honeymoon because we were still on Cloud Nine, and our life together was so new and sweet that living in a jungle would have been all right. But now we have two children and a lot more responsibility.

Kermit has been rather quiet since we talked about moving and I am feeling somewhat guilty for having thrown cold water on his enthusiasm. The happiness, dream and promise are gone from his eyes, but I am sure that God will help him to be happy here, too. Surely Kermit will get over it and our happy life will continue. Besides, we gave our word that we would rent this place for five years and that means it will be three more years before we can think of moving.

I won't give in, because I know that Kermit only wants what would make me happy, too. Oh, dear, what position does that put me in if I want to obey the Golden Rule and also want Kermit to be happy? I am too tired to think about it any more tonight, so I will close for now.

October 3

There was a frost this morning, so it is time to gather the butternut squash and pull out the frozen flower stalks. The children and I spent the day with Mom and Sis so we had a houseful of babies, including the ones they take care of whose mothers are in prison. I told Mom about the new Mullet farm and about Kermit's enthusiasm for renting it, and she seems as negative about the idea as I am. I am sure it would be hard for her to see her daughter and precious grandchildren move so far away.

October 10

Kermit still seemed rather remote and the light in his eyes seems to be absent, his laughter sobered, and the usual joy of adventurous comradeship gone. This afternoon I couldn't bear it any longer. While Hannah was taking her long afternoon nap, I put Baby in the infant carrier and strode down Forget-Me-Not Lane, across the stepping stones, and through the old orchard to see Aunt Miriam. Surely she would tell me that I have a right to my own desires and wishes in the matter, too.

She was alone in the kitchen, sitting at the sewing machine piecing a quilt. I found myself pouring out my tale of woe to a sympathetic listener. Afterward I asked her, "Do you think I'm wrong in holding on to my wishes about moving? Surely Kermit should consider my feelings, too."

Aunt Miriam gazed thoughtfully out the window for a few moments, then turned back to me and said, "I once heard the saying, 'A man's home is his castle.' I believe that is the truth because God planned it that way from the beginning. The man is the head of the home and his wife must fit herself into the blueprint of his dreams. If she doesn't and insists on having things her way instead of what her husband desires, she is a usurper to the throne, and I don't believe that usurpers are ever happy."

I felt downcast at her words, almost like a naughty schoolgirl, until I met her kind gaze. I then took heart again, saying, "But surely the wife has a right to her dreams even if they differ from his."

Aunt Miriam nodded. "You know that Kermit loves you and that if you don't yield he will give up his own dreams bit by bit and give in to you. But in doing so, both of you will be weakening the foundation of your life together. A wise woman will never let that happen."

I pondered this for a moment, thinking of how I had seen the bright dream fade from Kermit's eyes and of weakening foundations. But I was puzzled and asked her, "Tell me then, what is the answer when a husband and a wife want different things."

Aunt Miriam's smile was gentle as she replied, "The wife has a castle, too, a wonderful castle in which she reigns as a queen. It is strong and secure from without, but very fragile from within. She is the only one who can tear down that castle, for it is a living thing which must be nurtured and tended lovingly, or it will decay. A wife who is content to rule only within the bounds of her own castle can be gloriously happy. When she steps out of her domain, she is apt to be unhappy. God has given women a power that is noble, queenly, and good if rightly used. She remains in her castle only by accepting her husband's plan for their life together, and by seeking to nurture and lovingly build her own private castle strong and sure."

I wasn't quite sure what she meant by the castle, but an egg customer came just then and I headed for home knowing I did not want to stay away from home long while Hannah was sleeping.

On the way home it dawned on me what Aunt Miriam meant. The castle was the wife's love of her husband. His happiness, virtues, faults, dreams, and dislikes must be accepted and hallowed by her love because these things make up her own secret castle. She must tend it lovingly, and in so doing will add a glory to the home of her husband's choosing.

Suddenly, I made my decision. Kermit should be able to realize his dream of working in the outdoors under the big, blue sky. I hurried home, laid the sleeping baby in his crib, then headed out to the woodworking shop to see Kermit.

"Guess what!" I said gaily. "We're moving to Montana!"

The astonished look on Kermit's face was priceless. Then with one swift movement, he caught me and whirled me around jubilantly until I was breathless and laughing. But what he said next surprised me even more than being twirled around had.

"We are **not** moving to Montana. I love you for giving in to my dreams, but I could never be happy knowing you didn't want to be there. We'll stay right here and keep the woodworking going."

Then he was all business showing me the piece he was making and telling me about the latest orders that had come in. It was such a relief to see the happiness back in his eyes that I did not pursue the matter further. But there are five months left until spring when we would have to leave to travel west, and I mean to convince him that we should go. And this time I will have my own way! (Smiles)

January 1, New Year's Day

Snow! It reminds me of the snow-covered landscape in Montana. The swirls and mounds of beautiful, fluffy, white snow covering everything and the sleigh rides on the bobsled with bells jingling merrily. There are many nice things about winter: attending quiltings and comfort-knottings; hearing the screeching sound of carriage wheels on soft snow; skaters on the frozen pond, swirling and gliding over the smooth ice; breathing in frosty cold air and breathing out puffs of frosty whiteness; coming in from the cold and crowding close to the big, black range trying to absorb its warmth; warming your toes in the bake oven. My thoughts often travel to Tall Cedars Homestead and Beechwood Acres and the winters we had there.

Now a brand new year lies ahead of us and new and exciting adventures await us. It took me exactly two months to convince Kermit that we should move to Montana, and as soon as he gave his consent, I wrote a letter to the Mullets with our offer and a request to rent the farm. The return letter came last week. Now the deal is closed and in about three months we'll be moving!

Now I am actually very eager and happy about going and am looking forward to living on the big homestead near Swift River.

The house in Montana is large and is made of stone. It has a nice-sized kitchen with a big picture window looking out over the Swift River and the Swift River Valley. I can hardly wait to see it! Treva and Jared are here again and will help us pack, then will move back with us.

> **Bible Verse for today:** *". . . Let us run with patience the race that is set before us, looking unto Jesus, the author and finisher of our faith; who, for the joy that was set before him, endured the cross, despising the shame. . .." (Hebrews 12:1-2)*

February 11

I have reached the last entry of my journal and will fill it with bits and pieces about Hannah and Henry, and a prayer.

Hannah has grown into a very pretty little girl and is the sunshine of our home. She talks in complete sentences and loves to run out to Kermit to spend time in the woodworking shop. One of Preacher Emanuel's sons will be renting this place in March and will take on the woodworking business.

Henry is a sturdy seven-month-old and is very much a mama's baby. He is a chubby, placid, and pleasant little chap who loves to get around in his walker. He's our little sunshine, too.

Kermit is very eager to start our new life in Swift River, yet I believe that even for him spring and moving time will be here before we are ready. There is still so much to do.

Sadie came over tonight and babysat for us while Kermit and I went for a walk down Forget-Me-Not-Lane and on to the swinging bridge, admiring the myriad of stars in the dusky winter sky and the red glow of the sunset. Before too long we will be seeing bigger mountains, trees, and skies, and hearing coyotes howling. We will miss my family, Sadie, Aunt Miriam, and all the others, but we will make new friends in Swift River and will come back to visit.

— **The End** —